I0420364

U.S. COUNTERTERRORISM EFFORTS IN SYRIA: A WINNING STRATEGY?

HEARING

BEFORE THE

SUBCOMMITTEE ON TERRORISM, NONPROLIFERATION, AND TRADE

OF THE

COMMITTEE ON FOREIGN AFFAIRS
HOUSE OF REPRESENTATIVES

ONE HUNDRED FOURTEENTH CONGRESS

FIRST SESSION

SEPTEMBER 29, 2015

Serial No. 114–101

Printed for the use of the Committee on Foreign Affairs

Available via the World Wide Web: http://www.foreignaffairs.house.gov/ or
http://www.gpo.gov/fdsys/

U.S. GOVERNMENT PUBLISHING OFFICE

96–816PDF   WASHINGTON : 2015

For sale by the Superintendent of Documents, U.S. Government Publishing Office
Internet: bookstore.gpo.gov   Phone: toll free (866) 512–1800; DC area (202) 512–1800
Fax: (202) 512–2104   Mail: Stop IDCC, Washington, DC 20402–0001

COMMITTEE ON FOREIGN AFFAIRS

EDWARD R. ROYCE, California, *Chairman*

CHRISTOPHER H. SMITH, New Jersey	ELIOT L. ENGEL, New York
ILEANA ROS-LEHTINEN, Florida	BRAD SHERMAN, California
DANA ROHRABACHER, California	GREGORY W. MEEKS, New York
STEVE CHABOT, Ohio	ALBIO SIRES, New Jersey
JOE WILSON, South Carolina	GERALD E. CONNOLLY, Virginia
MICHAEL T. McCAUL, Texas	THEODORE E. DEUTCH, Florida
TED POE, Texas	BRIAN HIGGINS, New York
MATT SALMON, Arizona	KAREN BASS, California
DARRELL E. ISSA, California	WILLIAM KEATING, Massachusetts
TOM MARINO, Pennsylvania	DAVID CICILLINE, Rhode Island
JEFF DUNCAN, South Carolina	ALAN GRAYSON, Florida
MO BROOKS, Alabama	AMI BERA, California
PAUL COOK, California	ALAN S. LOWENTHAL, California
RANDY K. WEBER SR., Texas	GRACE MENG, New York
SCOTT PERRY, Pennsylvania	LOIS FRANKEL, Florida
RON DeSANTIS, Florida	TULSI GABBARD, Hawaii
MARK MEADOWS, North Carolina	JOAQUIN CASTRO, Texas
TED S. YOHO, Florida	ROBIN L. KELLY, Illinois
CURT CLAWSON, Florida	BRENDAN F. BOYLE, Pennsylvania
SCOTT DesJARLAIS, Tennessee	
REID J. RIBBLE, Wisconsin	
DAVID A. TROTT, Michigan	
LEE M. ZELDIN, New York	
DANIEL DONOVAN, New York	

AMY PORTER, *Chief of Staff*   THOMAS SHEEHY, *Staff Director*

JASON STEINBAUM, *Democratic Staff Director*

––––––––

SUBCOMMITTEE ON TERRORISM, NONPROLIFERATION, AND TRADE

TED POE, Texas, *Chairman*

JOE WILSON, South Carolina	WILLIAM KEATING, Massachusetts
DARRELL E. ISSA, California	BRAD SHERMAN, California
PAUL COOK, California	BRIAN HIGGINS, New York
SCOTT PERRY, Pennsylvania	JOAQUIN CASTRO, Texas
REID J. RIBBLE, Wisconsin	ROBIN L. KELLY, Illinois
LEE M. ZELDIN, New York	

CONTENTS

U.S. COUNTERTERRORISM EFFORTS IN SYRIA: A WINNING STRATEGY?

TUESDAY, SEPTEMBER 29, 2015

HOUSE OF REPRESENTATIVES,
SUBCOMMITTEE ON TERRORISM, NONPROLIFERATION, AND TRADE,
COMMITTEE ON FOREIGN AFFAIRS,
Washington, DC.

The subcommittee met, pursuant to notice, at 2 o'clock p.m., in room 2172 Rayburn House Office Building, Hon. Ted Poe (chairman of the subcommittee) presiding.

Mr. POE. The subcommittee will come to order. Without objection, all members may have 5 days to submit statements, questions, and extraneous materials for the record subject to the length limitation in the rules.

I will make my opening statement, then yield to the ranking member, Mr. Keating, for his statement.

On September 10th, 2014, President Obama announced that the United States would "degrade and ultimately destroy ISIS." That was a year ago. Obviously, ISIS didn't get the memo. The terrorist group keeps on moving across the Middle East killing those who stand in its way by raping, pillaging, and murdering those who disagree with ISIS.

ISIS controls half of Syria and large parts of Iraq. Civilized society is losing to these barbarians. Despite the U.S. spending billions in a counterterrorism strategy, the terrorist groups numbers have not decreased; in fact, ISIS has grown in size with affiliates now all over the world, including Indonesia, Yemen, Egypt, and Libya.

The U.S. $3.7 billion air strike campaign has been plagued with little measurable successful results. From the very beginning, military officials warned that the air strikes relied on virtually no human intelligence on the ground surveillance. They were right. Without good intelligence, the number of air strikes the U.S. has carried out have been few, and the results are uncertain. Also, ISIS fighters killed by our air strikes seem to be replaced immediately with other jihadists.

Our intelligence estimates that ISIS' numbers are the same as they were when the air strikes started. In addition, the administration's $500 million Train and Equip Program has proved to be a failure by anyone's measure. In July, officials reported they had identified 7,000 planned participants, but only trained 60 due to intense vetting procedures, and other excuses.

Later that month, 54 fighters crossed into Syria to fight ISIS forces that numbered in the tens of thousands. Of those 54 merce-

(1)

naries, virtually all were killed, captured, or scattered when attacked. We're now down to four or five trained mercenaries according to General Lloyd Austin of CENTCOM.

Despite this failed policy, just last week we sent a second group of about 70 U.S.-trained fighters into Syria. Just 1 day later, reports suggested that one of the officers defected and surrendered his arms to an al-Qaeda Syrian affiliate. Several truckloads of weapons were allegedly traded to the terrorist group al-Nusra for safe passage through Syria. It's time to abandoned this failed Train and Equip Program.

The reality is just as bleak on the online battlefield. ISIS has 30 to 40,000 social media accounts. It uses the internet to spread its propaganda, raise money, and find recruits as far away as Washington State. In 2011, the administration promised a strategy to combat terrorists' use of social media. Four years later, the administration still has not shown us that strategy; no plan, no degrading of ISIS, no defeating of ISIS.

The intel given to the administration has also reportedly been doctored to cover up how bad the war against ISIS is really going. Meanwhile, thousands of people are fleeing the Middle East, flooding Europe, and demanding entry into other Western countries because of the ISIS carnage and chaos in Syria and Iraq. There is more. ISIS continues to recruit want-to-be jihadists online for free via U.S.-owned social media companies.

The administration continually is saying that everything is okay, is an embarrassing and wrong assessment of the violence and threat of ISIS. Today, we are here to get frank assessment of the administration's counterterrorism strategy in Syria. In the face of our failure to destroy ISIS, we should be focusing on what we can do better, how we can improve our strategy in the future.

ISIS' advances in Syria translate into more direct threats to our national security and our interests both home and abroad. ISIS wants to destroy the United States and everything the U.S. stands for. ISIS fears no one; certainly not the U.S., so it continues to murder in the name of its radical jihadist beliefs. It has already killed numerous Americans. We need a strategy that protects American people from this radical Islamic threat. Now we hear on the horizon that the Russians may intervene and help defeat ISIS. Who knows?

The U.S. needs to define the enemy and defeat it. And that's the way it is, and I'll yield to the ranking member, Mr. Keating.

Mr. KEATING. Thank you, Mr. Chairman, for conducting this hearing, and I thank also our witnesses for being here today.

The conflict in Syria is an open wound in the volatile Middle East. President Assad has brutalized, bombed, used chemical weapons on his own people creating the conditions for ISIL and al-Qaeda to thrive in Syria, and driving millions of Syrians to flee their country. The resulting refugee crisis has severely strained the resources of Syria's neighbors and exposing divides in Europe, which in some parts is already suffering from an intolerant brand of nationalism.

The conflict in Syria is also drawing in foreign fighters who contribute to the instability and represent possible terrorist threats when they return to their countries of origin, including the United States. To put it mildly, the order of battle in Syria is complex.

The United States has called for Assad to leave power and opposes ISIL and al-Qaeda affiliate, al-Nusra. The United States supports so-called moderate Syrian opposition forces and the Syrian Kurdish group known as YPG. Meanwhile, our NATO ally, Turkey, late to the fight against ISIL opposes Assad and Kurdish militants, and the PKK, as well, which also has close ties to our Syrian Kurdish allies, the YPG. Our sometimes allies against ISIL, Iraq, Iran, and Russian support the Assad regime, and our partners in Saudi Arabia and the Gulf States oppose Assad and ISIL, while some individuals within these states provide funding to Sunni extremist groups in Syria.

Given this tangled regional situation which has been further complicated by Russia's recent movement of military equipment and personnel into Syria, the United States has, in my view, wisely refrained from introducing sizeable ground force into Syria to combat ISIL. Yet, in concert with our partners we must do more to counter and defeat ISIL which controls significant territory in Syria and Iraq, extending its influence beyond the Middle East into Africa and Asia.

ISIL's atrocities are horrific, and we must work to put a stop to its campaign of murder, slavery, and the destruction of cultural heritage. By virtue of its ideology, ISIL needs to control territory in order to survive, and to ultimately defeat ISIL we need to assist our allies in the region in retaking that territory.

The key questions in my mind are, how will the United States and its partners sufficiently array its forces against ISIL to defeat it? And as we work to do this, how will we deal with the Assad regime whose illegitimacy and brutality was the root cause of the Syrian civil war?

We know that to date the plan to train and equip moderate Syrian fighters has not met its objectives. I hope that today's hearing will provide some constructive proposals on how going forward the United States and its allies can enhance counterterrorism efforts in Syria.

I yield back, Mr. Chair.

Mr. POE. Thank the gentleman from Massachusetts.

The Chair recognizes the gentleman from South Carolina, Mr. Wilson, for 1 minute.

Mr. WILSON. Thank you, Mr. Chairman.

Sadly, the President's strategy in Syria is failing, resulting in refugees fleeing violence and then drowning at sea. According to a recent article in the New York Times, the administration reports,

> "That coalition strikes killed about 10,000 Islamic State fighters. The group continues to replenish its ranks drawing an average of about 1,000 new fighters per month."

The President was wrong to belittle ISIS to JV, and he was wrong and made a mockery of the term "red line." The failure of the Train and Equip mission of Syrian Opposition Forces has given enemy reinforcements space to insert itself and prop up the Assad dictatorship.

The U.S. needs to change course and create a new strategy to defeat safe havens threatening American families at home. I believe it's important that the U.S. and international community recognize that the situation in Iraq and Syria is, in fact, a global problem requiring broad international cooperation to promote stability in the region for families to prosper in their home nation.

Mr. POE. The gentleman yields back his time.

The Chair recognizes the gentleman from California, Mr. Sherman, for 1-minute opening statement.

Mr. SHERMAN. No one in the administration is saying that everything is okay. The Shiite Alliance is more dangerous than ISIS and more evil. They've killed far more Americans starting in the 1980s when Hezbollah attacked our Marines. And so if we confront ISIS, we have to do so in a way that does not empower Assad, Hezbollah, and Iran.

You can attack U.S. policy, but we don't as a nation want to send troops into the ground, and we are living with the results of an absolutely failed policy of the last administration in Iraq which installed Maliki, slightly improved now with al-Abadi. The fact is, the Iraqi Government betrayed us this week in entering into a special intelligence alliance with Iran, Assad, and Russia.

The Train and Equip Program has been a failure. Due to political correctness, we have not armed those we know are not Islamic extremists; namely, the Yazidis and the Christians. And due to diplomatic correctness, we have not armed the Kurds directly, but try to put everything through Baghdad. That does not mean we should abandon the Train and Equip Program, which should have begun much earlier, as many on this committee argued, because what is the alternative? The chairman tells us we must defeat ISIS. Whose ground troops are going to do that, and what is a plan other than the administration's plan, poorly carried out in the case of the Train and Equip Program, that will allow us to achieve that goal without massive American casualties.

I yield back.

Mr. POE. The gentleman's time has expired.

The Chair recognizes the gentleman from Pennsylvania, Mr. Perry, for 1 minute.

Mr. PERRY. Thank you, Mr. Chairman.

In spite of its shortcomings, and there are many, the last administration's policy was not completely failed, and I would submit that the failure was after that President left, and with the advent of the new policy.

To that effect, in his September 2014 address from the White House, President Obama laid out a plan to degrade and ultimately destroy ISIL through a comprehensive and sustained counterterrorism strategy. In Syria, this goal was to be achieved with two major policies; a systematic campaign of air strikes and increased support to forces fighting the Islamic State on the ground.

A year later, what does this strategy currently look like? Eleven sorties per day yielding an average of 43 bombs dropped daily, a handful of Syrian rebels who would rather be fighting Assad at a cost of about $100 million to the American taxpayer.

According to a report published recently by the Syrian Observatory for Human Rights, ISIS has extended its territorial reach and now controls 50 percent of Syria, including most of the country's oil wells which have proven to be a significant source of revenue.

Mr. Chairman, I think it is high time this administration go back to the drawing board.

I yield back.

Mr. POE. The gentleman yields back his time.

The Chair recognizes the gentleman, Mr. Rohrabacher, for 1 minute.

Mr. ROHRABACHER. Thank you very much, Mr. Chairman.

This administration has managed to turn a bad situation, which it did inherit, which was a bad situation that we created on this side of the aisle by going along with the President who precipitously invaded Iraq at a time when he hadn't finished in Afghanistan, but that bad situation this administration inherited has been turned into a catastrophe of this administration's making.

U.S. policies, even our supplies sent to defeat ISIL are now in the possession of radical Islamic groups that intend on killing Americans and other people who believe in our Western values. This administration has found every excuse to undermine the governments and the forces that are most friendly to our cause and the cause of peace.

In Syria, we refused to cooperate with Russia 5 years ago claiming that there was an alternative, and what happened in those 5 years? It's turned into an ever-worse situation, and the money that was sent over to arm a Third Force we now find has been used to train and equip hostile forces to those people who are trying to bring peace to the Middle East.

Thank you for holding this hearing; looking forward to getting the details.

Mr. POE. The gentleman yields back.

The Chair will now recognize and introduce all three of our witnesses. Thank you, gentlemen, for being here.

General Jack Keane is the chairman of the board at the Institute of the Study of War. General Keane is a retired four-star general and the former vice-chief of staff for the United States Army.

Mr. Thomas Joscelyn is a senior fellow at the Foundation for Defense of Democracies, and senior editor of The Long War Journal, a publication dealing with counterterrorism and related issues.

And Ambassador Daniel Benjamin is director of the John Sloan Dickey Center for International Understanding at Dartmouth. Ambassador Benjamin previously served as Ambassador-at-Large and coordinator for the counterterrorism at the United States State Department.

Thank you, gentlemen, for being here. General Keane, we'll start with you.

STATEMENT OF GENERAL JACK KEANE, USA, RETIRED, CHAIRMAN OF THE BOARD, INSTITUTE FOR THE STUDY OF WAR

General KEANE. Thank you, Chairman Poe, Ranking Member Keating, distinguished members of the committee for inviting me back today. I'm honored to be here with my distinguished panel colleagues.

The Middle East has experienced one of the most tumultuous periods in its history with the old order challenged by the aspirational goals of the Arab Spring, Islamic terrorists taking advantage of this political and social upheaval, and Iran using proxies to achieve regional influence and control.

ISIS has become the most successful terrorist organization in modern history by dominating a large swath of Syrian-Iraq territory while expanding its formal affiliations into seven countries, and developing a worldwide following.

As you mentioned, Mr. Chairman, approximately a year ago, the President announced U.S. policy that in conjunction with our Coalition partners we would degrade, and ultimately defeat ISIS. While there has been some progress, looking at this strategy today, we now know the conceptual plan of Iraq first and minimal commitment in Syria is fundamentally flawed. The resources provided to support Iraq and Syria are far from adequate. The indigenous ground forces in Syria and Iraq are not capable of defeating ISIS. The air campaign rules of engagement are too restrictive. We have not impacted the ideology or ISIS recruiting as 28,000 new recruits have arrived this year alone. As such, we are not only failing, we are losing this war. I can say with certainty our strategy will not defeat ISIS.

ISIS, who is headquartered in Syria, recruits, trains, and re-supplies in Syria. It is from Syria that ISIS has so successfully expanded, and it is from Syria that ISIS reaches out to 20,000 social media sites per day. They control large swaths of territory in Syria from Iraq border to Damascus. This territorial control is what differentiates it from other terrorist organizations, but it is also its greatest vulnerability.

To defeat ISIS, we must take its territory away, as we did with Germany, Japan, and Korea; yet, we have no strategy to defeat ISIS in Syria. We have no effective ground force, which is a defeat mechanism. Air power will not defeat ISIS; it has not even been able to deny ISIS the ability to attack at will. ISIS grew to a terrorist army only because of the sanctuary in Syria. We cannot succeed in Iraq if ISIS is allowed to exist in Syria.

The United States finds itself at a critical juncture with its ISIS strategy failing, the Syrian civil war in its fourth year, and because the Assad regime this last year has been losing ground to the rebels and some political support, Vladimir Putin is executing a military buildup in Syria to insure the survival of the Assad regime. Putin is also working to create an alternative anti-ISIS Coalition that includes Russia, Iran, Syria, and Iraq in a direct challenge to the U.S.-led Coalition.

In view of these very real challenges, what can we do? As to the strategy, Sun Tzu said, "Tactics without a strategy is the noise before defeat," and we have some noise.

Once and for all, 22 years after the first World Trade Center bombing, 14 years after 9/11, we should develop in conjunction with our allies a comprehensive strategy to defeat radical Islam. Otherwise, we will continue to react to individual terrorist movements, al-Qaeda, ISIS, Ansar al-Sharia, Boko Haram, you name it, with no end in sight.

As to Syria, recognizing an effective ground force is the key to defeating ISIS with much less restrictive use of air power. The ground force should consist of the Syria Kurds, the only force who has enjoyed success against ISIS in Syria. This force should be armed as required, and provided special forces advisors to assist with the use of air power.

Despite the dismal failure of the Train and Equip mission of the moderate Sunni Arab Force, I agree with Mr. Sherman, it is still essential to put together this vital capability. The parameters for this force must change. We cannot restrict the Sunni Syrian Arabs to exclusively fighting ISIS, when their priority is the Assad regime who is destroying their communities and killing their families. They want to fight the Assad regime and ISIS; let them.

Also, this force and their communities must be protected as should the Syria Kurds. Begin by establishing free zones in the north and south, use Coalition air power to include the Turks to enforce it, and permit the people to use the free zone as a sanctuary. Advise Assad if he challenges the free zone, then U.S.-led Coalition will shut down his air power.

We must step up the use of our special operations forces to conduct routine ground raids, not just limited to drone raids. But the harsh reality is that the Syrian Kurds and the Sunni Arabs may not be sufficient to dislodge ISIS and defeat them in Syria. And the task may ultimately require an outside Arab coalition assisted by the United States ground and air components.

As to Assad, while the United States and the Coalition desires a political solution to the Syrian civil war, recognize that Assad will never depart unless the military momentum shifts against him. Despite Russia's military pressure, this should still be U.S. policy.

As to Russia, once again, Putin is outmaneuvering the United States, and once again he will out-bluff us. Putin's economy is in the tank. His financial reserves are running out. His military is no match against the United States. He has deployed a relatively small military and limited capability to Syria; yet, he will likely get what he wants, the preservation of the Assad regime.

The United States should not coordinate any military operations with Russia. To do so, we are de facto in collusion with the Syrian regime, Iran, the Quds Force, and Hezbollah. Putin is counting on President Obama's fear of escalation, and fear of confrontation to force U.S. capitulation to Russia's ambition in Syria, and the Middle East at large. This, in my view, is a game changer.

There are no easy answers in Syria, but we don't have the luxury to say it's too hard, and it's too complicated. There have been plenty of mistakes and lost opportunities to be sure, but U.S. interests, U.S. security, and U.S. credibility is at stake. What is most needed now is U.S. determined leadership and resolve to commit to defeating ISIS along with a revised effective strategy.

Thank you, and I look forward to your questions.

[The prepared statement of General Keane follows:]

Testimony

United States House of Representatives

House Committee on Foreign Affairs
Subcommittee on Terrorism, Nonproliferation, and Trade

By

General John M. Keane, USA (Ret)

on

U.S. Counterterrorism Efforts in Syria: A Winning Strategy?

1400 hours, 29 September 2015

Rayburn House Office Building

Room 2172

Thank you Chairman Poe, ranking member Keating, distinguished members of the committee for inviting me today to discuss U.S. strategy in Syria. Am honored to be with my distinguished colleagues Thomas Joscelyn and Daniel Benjamin.

The Middle East is experiencing one of the most tumultuous periods in its history with the old order challenged by the aspirational goals of the Arab Spring, radicalized Islamic terrorists taking advantage of the political and social upheaval and the Islamic state of Iran using proxies to achieve regional influence and control.

ISIS, an off-shoot from Al Qaeda in Iraq, has become the most successful terrorist organization in modern history by dominating a large swath of Syrian and Iraq territory while expanding its affiliations into 7 other countries and developing a worldwide following.

Approximately a year ago, the President announced the U.S. public policy that in conjunction with our coalition partners, the U.S. would degrade and ultimately destroy ISIS, weeks later he changed destroy ISIS to defeat ISIS, a more appropriate term.

A strategy was crafted to accomplish this objective which consisted of humanitarian assistance, undermining the ISIS religious ideology, countering the ISIS finances, providing military assistance to our Iraqi and Syrian partners to include airstrikes, assisting the Iraq government politically to move to a more representative government and continuing the policy supporting the removal of Assad.

While there has been some progress and some success, looking at this strategy today we, now, know:

- the conceptual plan is fundamentally flawed.

- the resources provided to support Iraq and Syria are far from adequate.

- the timing and urgency to provide arms, equipment and training is insufficient.

- the indigenous ground forces in Syria and Iraq are not capable of defeating ISIS.

- the air campaign rules of engagement are too restrictive.

As such, we are not only failing, we are losing this war, moreover I can say with certainty this strategy will not defeat ISIS.

ISIS who is headquartered in Syria, recruits, trains and resupplies in Syria. It is from Syria that ISIS has so successfully expanded and it is from Syria that ISIS reaches out to 20K social media sites per day. They control large swaths of territory in Syria to include the Euphrates River Valley, which connects to the Euphrates in Anbar Province, Iraq, which they also now control. This controlled territory is currently expanding to the west as far as Damascus and includes, Palmyra city and Palmyra airbase in central Syria, aligning the central East/West corridor from the Iraq border to Homs in western Syria. ISIS control of territory is what differentiates it from other terrorist organizations, but it is its greatest vulnerability. To defeat ISIS, we must take its territory away. Yet, we have no strategy to defeat ISIS in Syria, we have no effective ground force, which is the defeat mechanism. Yes, we have air power and yes we have degraded the command and control, logistics, and killed many ISIS fighters and despite the success at Kobani, air power will not defeat ISIS, it has not even been able to deny ISIS freedom of maneuver and the ability to attack at will. Syria is an ISIS sanctuary, without which ISIS would be a much smaller, yet violent, terrorist organization operating in the shadows in Iraq. ISIS grew to a terrorist army only because of the sanctuary in Syria. We cannot succeed in Iraq if ISIS is allowed to exist in Syria.

The U.S. finds itself at a critical juncture, with its ISIS strategy failing, in Syria and in Iraq, the Syrian civil war is in its fourth year and while the Bashar al Assad regime this last year has been losing ground to the rebels with some erosion of Alawite support, Vladimir Putin, is executing a military buildup in Syria to insure the survival of the Assad regime. Putin is also working to create an alternative anti-ISIS coalition that includes Russia, Iran and the Syrian regime in a direct challenge to the U.S. led coalition currently active against ISIS in Syria and Iraq.

In view of these very real challenges what can we do?

-Strategy:

Sun Tzu said: ". . . tactics without a strategy is the noise before defeat." Once and for all, 22 years after the first World Trade Center bombing and 14 years after 9/11, develop in conjunction with our allies a comprehensive strategy to defeat radical Islam. Otherwise we will continue to react to individual movements, e.g. AQ, ISIS, AAS etc, with no end in sight.

-Syria:

Recognize that an effective ground force is the key to defeating ISIS with a much less restrictive use of air power to support the ground force. The ground force in the near term should consist of the Syrian Kurds (the only force who has enjoyed success against ISIS in Syria.) This force should be armed as required and provided special forces advisers to assist with the use of air power. Despite the dismal failure of the train and equip mission of the moderate Sunni Arab force, it is still essential to put together this vital capability. The parameters for this force must change. We cannot restrict the Sunni Arabs to exclusively fighting ISIS when their priority is the Assad regime who is destroying their communities and killing their families. They want to fight the Assad regime and ISIS, let them. Also, the force and their communities must be protected as should the Syrian Kurds. Begin by establishing free zones (FZ) in the north and south near the Turkish and Jordanian borders. Use coalition air power to include the Turks to enforce it and permit the people to use the FZ as a sanctuary. Advise Assad, if he challenges the FZ, then the U.S. led coalition will shut down his air power.

We must step up the use of special operations forces (SOF) to conduct routine ground and drone raids on ISIS leadership which was so successful in Iraq and Afghanistan. These raids at times should be expanded to a 2 or 3 day operation using Army Rangers to destroy key nodes and capabilities.

The harsh reality is that the Syrian Kurds and Sunni Arabs may not be sufficient to dislodge ISIS and defeat them in Syria and the task may require an outside Arab coalition assisted by the U.S. ground and air components.

-Assad:

While the U.S. and the coalition desires a political solution to the Syrian civil war, recognize that Assad will never depart unless the military momentum shifts against him. Despite Russia's military pressure this should still be U.S. policy.

-Russia:

Once again Putin is out maneuvering the U.S. and once again he will out bluff us. The U.S. should not coordinate any military operations with Russia. To do so means we are de facto in collusion with the Syrian regime, Iran, the Quds force and the Hezbollah. Putin knows full well his military is no match for the U.S. and NATO. He is counting on President Obama's fear of escalation to force U.S. capitulation to Russia's ambition in Syria and the Middle East at large.

There are no easy answers in Syria, there have been plenty of mistakes and lost opportunities to be sure, but U.S. interests and U.S. credibility is at stake. What is most needed now is U.S. determined leadership and resolve to commit to defeating ISIS, along with a revised effective strategy.

Thank you, and I look forward to your questions.

———

Mr. POE. Thank you. Mr. Joscelyn.

STATEMENT OF MR. THOMAS JOSCELYN, SENIOR FELLOW, FOUNDATION FOR DEFENSE OF DEMOCRACIES

Mr. JOSCELYN. Chairman Poe, Ranking Member Keating, and other members of the committee, thank you for inviting me here today to speak about our counterterrorism efforts in Syria.

As others have already said, the war is exceedingly complex. I'm not going to pretend to have all the answers for you, but I've heard a few things here already which are consistent with my testimony. I want to highlight them in my oral testimony.

First is sort of the necessity of removing territory from the Islamic State or ISIS. The Kurds have done a good job this year taking the northern third of Raqqah Province away from the Islamic State, but as David Ignatius in the Washington Post recently reported, they've been basically under-resourced, and for some reason there's a holdup in getting more resources to take that fight to Islamic State. I don't know why that is; however, that seems to be the case.

In that vein, I would say that the founding mythos of the Islamic State is that it is the resurrection of the Caliphate. They brought this back to being a reality on this earth. And I think that as long as that myth exists and lives, that basically we're going to keep seeing more recruitment, we're going to keep seeing more people flock to the Caliphate. Now, you're going to have some people who defect, and who aren't happy, and who go home, and we need to trumpet their messages. But as long as this founding myth that they are the Caliphate and control territory exists, they're going to keep going.

And to that point, this morning the Treasury Department released what I think is really unprecedented; 35 terrorist designations at once this morning. Most of the designations deal with the Islamic State and underscore the degree to which the Islamic State has mushroomed. They deal with the Islamic State's provinces in the in the Khorasan and the Caucus Province, also the Islamic State's growing presence in the Sinai. And also, most importantly, deals with western recruits have gone to the Islamic State and posed some level of threat to their home countries.

Now, the plots that have been, I think, highlighted in these designations aren't necessarily 9/11 style plots. These aren't these sort of spectacular events that we should all be worried about, but it shows that there is at least the seed of an idea of attacking their home countries there with some of the individuals who were designated this morning.

One quick point to something Mr. Sherman said about Iran and Assad. I think even taking it a step further, I think that they actually are the fundamental destabilizing force in the region, and have actually fueled Sunni jihadism. Just last month, as we reported in The Long War Journal, the Islamic State brutally executed four members of the popular mobilization forces in Iraq. They did so in a manner that was consistent with the way the Shiite extremists had previously executed Sunnis who they were fighting. And too oftentimes in our media coverage, we get the ISIS video which is sort of, you know, glossy and highly stylized, and something that's really there for the wow factor, but not enough attention is given to what's happening on the Shiite side which is really driving this. And, unfortunately, as long as Shiite extremism is expanding, what that does is it forces Sunnis more into the radicals camps, more into the jihadist camps, and that's not a good thing. Obviously, that underscores the idea that in the long run, Assad and Iran are not an answer to this at all.

One further threat stream that I want to highlight today, and this goes to a lot of what we work on. I think it's very poorly misunderstood, is the al-Nusra Front, and the Sunni jihadists in Syria who are not aligned with the Islamic State, and who are actually opposed to them. I think they're actually—there's a gross misunderstanding of what they're doing, because what you don't hear often is that they are actually building their own state in northern Syria, and particularly in the Idlib Province.

The al-Nusra Front is openly loyal to Ayman al-Zawahiri, the head of al-Qaeda. It is seeded with senior al-Qaeda operatives, some of whom have actually trained, and lived, and worked with al-Qaeda going back to the 1980s. In a recent video, they highlighted the 9/11 attacks as something that's part of their legacy and their heritage, and say that this is part of—they're the heirs of this glory. And their videos and propaganda show very clearly that al-Qaeda actually seeks to build an Islamic State or Emirate as well in Syria. This is absolutely without a doubt.

And, in fact, is you look at the Train and Equip Program, the recent problems with it, I think this is another fact that needs to be highlighted. The problems came not from ISIS, the problems came from al-Nusra Front or al-Qaeda, going back to July when members of Division 30 went into Syria into the Aleppo Province, it was al-Nusra that was waiting for them that, as you said, Chairman Poe, killed, and captured, and basically disbanded this group very quickly. We were not expecting that for some reason on the U.S. side.

Now just recently we have now an admission from CENTCOM saying that, in fact, several vehicles and ammunition at a minimum were turned over to al-Nusra Front in northern Syria, not ISIS, as part of a deal that was brokered to basically guarantee safe passage for some of the people who were somehow affiliated with this program.

I think this highlights to a certain extent that there's such a myopic focus on the Islamic State, and such a drive to say the Islamic State is really the only threat we have to be worried about here, that basically a lot of times what's actually happening with these other groups is just as important, if not more so in the long run.

And finally I'll say this, there's been somewhat of a public relations campaign to get the West to support or at least tactically support some of the Sunni jihadists in Syria, including Ahrar al-Sham. That is a horrible idea. Members of the Obama administration have actually openly objected to that idea and said that's a no-go. They are right in that regard. Ahrar al-Sham should in no way be our partner in Syria. They cannot be. This is a group that openly says that the Mullah Omar's Taliban is a model for what they're building in Syria. It is deeply allied with al-Qaeda in Syria. It's had senior al-Qaeda veterans implanted in its ranks, and seeded in its ranks. This is a group that is absolutely not worthy of our support, and so I will end on a final warning; which is that the Sunni jihadists who are not Islamic State, and are not affiliated, and are actually against Assad, a lot of these groups are not our allies.

[The prepared statement of Mr. Joscelyn follows:]

Congressional Testimony

"U.S. Counterterrorism Efforts in Syria: A Winning Strategy?"

Thomas Joscelyn
Senior Fellow, Foundation for Defense of Democracies
Senior Editor, The Long War Journal

**Hearing before House Committee on Foreign Affairs
Subcommittee on Terrorism, Nonproliferation, and Trade**

Washington, DC
September 29, 2015

FOUNDATION FOR
DEFENSE OF DEMOCRACIES   1726 M Street NW • Suite 700 • Washington, DC 20036

Chairman Poe, Ranking Member Keating, and other members of the committee, thank you for inviting me here today to speak about America's counterterrorism efforts in Syria.

The war in Syria is exceedingly complex, with multiple actors fighting one another on the ground and foreign powers supporting their preferred proxies. Iran and Hezbollah are backing Bashar al Assad's regime, which is also now receiving increased assistance from Russia. The Islamic State (often referred to by the acronyms ISIS and ISIL) retains control over a significant amount of Syrian territory. Despite some setbacks at the hands of the U.S.-led air coalition and Kurdish ground forces earlier this year in northern Syria, Abu Bakr al Baghdadi's organization has not suffered anything close to a knockout blow thus far. Sunni jihadists, led by Al Nusrah Front and its closest allies, are opposed to both the Islamic State and the Assad regime. Unfortunately, they have been the most effective anti-Assad forces for some time, as could be seen in their stunning advances in the Idlib province earlier this year. Turkey, Qatar, Saudi Arabia and other nations are all sponsoring proxies in the fight.

Given the complexity of the war in Syria, it should be obvious that there are no easy answers. We were asked to assess whether or not the U.S. and its allies have a winning strategy. I would argue that there currently is no comprehensive strategy in place. The West's involvement is ad hoc, tactical and reactionary. Consider the recent news, confirmed by CENTCOM, that some of the equipment and ammunition supplied to U.S.-backed rebels has been turned over to the Al Nusrah Front, which is an arm of al Qaeda. These provisions were supposed to be used in the fight against the Islamic State, Al Nusrah's bitter jihadist rival. But Al Nusrah interfered in the plan. And this isn't the first time al Qaeda got in the way. In July, Al Nusrah quickly disbanded a small cadre of more than 50 fighters who were inserted into Syria to fight the Islamic State. In both cases, U.S. officials either did not know that Al Nusrah was likely to move against America's proxies, or assumed that Al Nusrah wouldn't. This demonstrates a lack of strategic thinking, as the train and equip program was so focused on the Islamic State that U.S. officials had not properly accounted for Al Nusrah's entirely predictable actions.

My testimony below is focused on the ideas that I think should inform our strategic thinking about the Syrian war. It is far from comprehensive. To my mind, three main points stand out:

(1) Any strategy for truly defeating the Islamic State needs to incorporate plans for clearing and holding large areas currently under its control. Thus far, no ground forces have been capable of doing this in cities such as Raqqa and Mosul, which are key to the Islamic State's "caliphate" claim. There is opposition to the Islamic State in these areas. For instance, the Kurds have delivered some significant losses on the Islamic State in northern Syria and have come within 30 miles of its de facto capital this year.

(2) Iran has escalated the conflict and Iranian influence is inherently destabilizing the entire region. Iran supports both Bashar al Assad's regime and the Iraqi government, but it does so by sponsoring Shiite extremism, which is no bulwark against Sunni extremism. Instead, the increasing role of Shiite extremists backed by Iran is driving more Sunnis into the jihadists' arms. This is precisely the opposite of what any strategist should want. Iran's proxies are not capable of clearing and holding territory from the Islamic State or

al Qaeda. And even if they were, this would only further strengthen the hand of Iran's virulent anti-American revolution.

(3) Some have advocated working with Sunni jihadists in Syria, but this would play right into al Qaeda's hands. Groups such as Al Nusrah Front and Ahrar al Sham have long been working to inculcate jihadism within the Syrian population. They are using the vicious war to spread their radical ideology, which is a different strain of jihadism from the Islamic State's belief system, but no less of a threat. In some ways, in fact, their version of jihadism may be a bigger long-term threat.

Below, I discuss these points and others in more detail.

The Islamic State's claim to rule as a "caliphate" will remain viable as long as it retains control over a significant amount of territory.

The Islamic State's founding mythos is that Abu Bakr al Baghdadi and his men have resurrected the "caliphate." For the Islamic State's base of supporters, this idea is a building block for their beliefs.[1] Two cities are particularly important for the Islamic State's "caliphate" claim: Raqqa and Mosul. Indeed, Baghdadi's only public appearance as the self-declared "Caliph Ibrahim" came when he led prayers in a Mosul mosque days after his men marauded through the city. Raqqa is the de facto capital of the "caliphate" and an operational nerve center for its nascent state. While the Islamic State's control of these two cities and other territory does not make it a true "caliphate," it is enough to continue fueling that perception among its supporters.

Controlling territory is crucially important for the Islamic State and its prospects for the future. The group's motto is: "Remaining and Expanding." The meaning is self-evident: the "caliphate" will remain in control of the lands it has conquered and will continue to seize new turf. The 5th edition of Dabiq, the Islamic State's English-language magazine, is devoted to this theme. The editors of Dabiq are anything but modest, stating that the Islamic State seeks nothing less than to "expand" until its "blessed flag…covers all eastern and western extents of the Earth, filling the world with the truth and justice of Islam and putting an end to the falsehood and tyranny of jahiliyyah [state of ignorance], even if American and its coalition despise such." Mecca, Medina, Rome, and Jerusalem -- all will fall to the Islamic State, if you believe its propagandists.

Of course, this is not possible. The Islamic State is not going to conquer Italy, Israel, and Saudi Arabia. Still, a lot of carnage and chaos has been wrought in pursuit of this imperialist dream. Until the Islamic State's claim to be "remaining and expanding" is conclusively disproven, too many people will continue to believe that it really is a "caliphate." And Baghdadi's men will retain some legitimacy in the minds of many of their recruits.

---

[1] This belief is, of course, not the only cause of radicalization among foreign fighters. Radicalization is a complicated psychological phenomenon. However, this belief is a much more powerful motivator than some believe. Dabiq magazine and other propaganda published by the Islamic State also contain apocalyptic themes. Baghdadi's followers are frequently told that a key battle awaits them in northern Syria, one that will decide the fate of the world. Should the Islamic State lose significant territory in Syria, then this theme will be largely discredited as well, as it will become apparent that Baghdadi's organization is not prepared to win this supposedly history-changing battle.

Therefore, the Islamic State cannot truly be "defeated" until it can no longer plausibly claim to rule over a large swath of territory. Its founding myth must be shattered. This does not require dislodging the Islamic State from all of the territory its black banner flies over. Indeed, Baghdadi's nascent nation has already lost some turf, including in the northern part of the Raqqa province. But high-profile losses, ones that cannot be denied by even the most ardent believer, are a must for any strategy to succeed in the long run. Ideally, Raqqa or Mosul would fall to the Islamic State's opposition. However, neither city appears to be under imminent threat.

The Islamic State's "caliphate" claim has other vulnerabilities that can be exploited. Its prolific media machine recently released a series of videos in various languages denouncing refugees fleeing Syria and Iraq. The refugees would receive "justice" under the Islamic State's laws, Baghdadi's propagandists claimed. While many of the refugees are fleeing Bashar al Assad's barrel bombs and other war crimes, it is undeniable that many are running away from the Islamic State's "caliphate" as well. In fact, the videos show that the Islamic State is concerned about the loss of human capital. Suicide bombers are not enough to man hospitals and food markets, or to provide other basic services. Indeed, there is much discontent among the Islamic State's residents already, as the "caliphate" is better at fighting than governing. To date, however, no force has been able to harness the populace's dissatisfaction.

Killing senior leaders and striking other high-value targets is not enough to defeat the Islamic State or al Qaeda.

In June 2006, the founder of al Qaeda in Iraq (AQI), Abu Musab al Zarqawi, was killed. It made little operational difference to the overall insurgency then raging in Iraq. The new leaders of AQI, Abu Hamza al Muhajir (a.k.a. Abu Ayyub al Masri) and Abu Omar al Baghdadi, were taken out in April 2010. At the time, under relentless pressure from coalition forces, the prospects for AQI and its political front, the Islamic State of Iraq (ISI), had dimmed. The targeting of AQI/ISI's leadership was combined with a robust counterinsurgency strategy that successfully forced the group from its strongholds and suppressed its ability to challenge the Iraqi government's sovereignty.

Still, AQI/ISI wasn't defeated. Abu Bakr al Baghdadi was appointed as the new leader and oversaw the group's resurrection, beginning with increasingly lethal attacks throughout 2012 (after the last American forces were withdrawn from Iraq in December 2011), a surge into Syria in 2013 (including the capture of Raqqa), and a stunningly successful offensive in Iraq in 2014 (culminating in the capture of Mosul). In late June 2014 – more than eight years after Zarqawi was killed – Abu Bakr al Baghdadi declared himself to be "Caliph Ibrahim" and his organization was rebranded as a "caliphate" known simply as the Islamic State.

There are plenty of other examples of jihadist groups surviving so-called decapitation strikes or significant leadership attrition. In September 2014, the al Qaeda-linked Ahrar al Sham lost much of its senior leadership in a mysterious explosion. Not only did Ahrar al Sham survive, today it thrives, leading the charge on Syrian battlefields. In Yemen, several of al Qaeda in Arabian Peninsula's (AQAP) top leaders have been killed since January. This includes Nasir al Wuhayshi, who was not only AQAP's emir, but also one of the most senior figures in al Qaeda's management team. This has not stopped AQAP's insurgency. The organization is more prolific than ever inside Yemen, capturing significant territory in the southern part of the country. Al Qaeda's senior leadership itself has survived the death of Osama bin Laden, as well as dozens of his and Ayman al Zawahiri's subordinates. With the exception of the Islamic State, al Qaeda's regional branches (discussed below) remain loyal to Zawahiri and al Qaeda is still closely allied with the Taliban.

There are a variety of reasons why jihadist groups typically survive senior leadership losses. These organizations are not structured like pyramids, with a few important figures making all of the important decisions on a day-to-day basis. They have, for practical reasons, evolved more efficient leadership structures, with significant responsibilities being given to the second and third tiers of their leadership cadres. In July, for instance, *The New York Times* cited "American and Iraqi intelligence officials" as saying that Abu Bakr al Baghdadi "has empowered his inner circle of deputies as well as regional commanders in Syria and Iraq with wide-ranging authority." This is part of the Islamic State's "plan to ensure that if he or other top figures are killed, the organization will quickly adapt and continue fighting."[2]

The current U.S. effort against both the Islamic State and al Qaeda is focused mainly on killing the most visible leaders in both organizations. The U.S. air campaign against the Islamic State in Iraq and Syria has also taken out numerous Islamic State fighting positions, weaponry, warehouses, explosives factories, and other important targets. But this is not sufficient to make the Islamic State crumble.

High-value targeting is most effective when it is combined with other counterinsurgency measures, clearing the territory held by the insurgents, holding it, and instituting new governance structures. Unfortunately, there are currently no boots on the ground truly capable of implementing a large-scale counterinsurgency strategy.

There are friendly forces fighting the Islamic State, but it is not clear if they would be capable of making more significant advances on the "caliphate's" territory. For example, the Kurds and their allies have taken the top third of the Raqqa province. In late June, the YPG (or People's Defense Units), announced that the town of Ain Issa had been "liberated." This is just 30 miles north of the city of Raqqa, which is the "caliphate's" de facto capital. For some reason, however, there have been delays in providing the Kurds with additional assistance.[3] Even if that assistance flows more readily, clearing and holding Raqqa would be a Herculean undertaking. Further complicating matters, some of the non-Kurdish forces fighting the Islamic State in Raqqa province have dubious pasts, with connections to al Qaeda's efforts in the country.

---

[2] Eric Schmitt and Ben Hubbard, "ISIS Leader Takes Steps to Ensure Group's Survival," *The New York Times*, July 20, 2015. (http://www.nytimes.com/2015/07/21/world/middleeast/isis-strategies-include-lines-of-succession-and-deadly-ring-tones.html)

[3] David Ignatius, "White House dithering paralyzes U.S.'s best ally for fighting the Islamic State," *The Washington Post*, September 22, 2015. (https://www.washingtonpost.com/opinions/white-house-dithering-paralyzes-uss-best-ally-for-fighting-the-islamic-state/2015/09/22/ba8fe4be-6151-11e5-8e9e-dce8a2a2a679_story.html)

The Iraqi and Syrian governments, backed by Iran and Russia, are not capable of waging a true counterinsurgency campaign. In fact, their actions have, in many ways, contributed to the rise of the Islamic State, Al Nusrah Front and other Sunni jihadist groups. Iranian-sponsored extremism is fuel for the war.

Sunni jihadists thrive off of sectarianism. And Shiite extremists are no true bulwark against Sunni extremists. In Iraq, Prime Minister Maliki's government shunned cooperation with the Sunni forces that could have been an incredibly valuable ally against the Islamic State early on. The dismantling of the Sunni "Awakening" and the failure to integrate its fighters into the Iraqi government's official security apparatus helped pave the way for the "caliphate's" surge in Iraq in 2014. Incredibly, the U.S.-backed Sunni coalition that did so much damage to al Qaeda in Iraq was treated like a pariah by the Iraqi government. As Derek Harvey and Michael Pregent have written, "The vast system of security forces and Sunni tribal auxiliaries that had made the Sunni provinces of Iraq hostile territory for al Qaeda was dismantled."[4] Maliki placed Shiites loyal to him and his cause in key positions. This "Shiafication" of the Iraqi military and security forces was "less about the security of Iraq than the security of Baghdad and [Maliki's] regime," Harvey and Pregent explained.

A key beneficiary of this "Shiafication" in Iraq is the Iranian regime, its Revolutionary Guard Corps (IRGC) and Hezbollah. Iran sponsors the Shiite militias that have often taken the lead in fighting the Islamic State in Iraq. These militias are not stabilizing Iraqi society – quite the opposite. Even though the U.S.-led coalition provides air cover for these militias, there is convincing evidence that they are brutalizing the population after driving the Islamic State's jihadists out.[5] The Iranian sponsored Shiite extremists are, in fact, committing many of the same war crimes that the Islamic State has become infamous for. A key reminder of this fact came in August, when the Islamic State burned four men alive. The Islamic State said the men belonged to the Popular Mobilization Forces (PMF). The grotesque execution was actually retribution for a similar act carried out by a Shiite extremist known as Abu Azrael (The "Father of the Angel of Death").[6]

The Popular Mobilization Committee (PMC) oversees the forces that Abu Azrael helps lead. The PMC is directed by Abu Mahdi al Muhandis, a former commander in the Badr Organization who was listed by the U.S. government as a specially designated global terrorist in July 2009.[7] The U.S. government described Muhandis, whose real name is Jamal Jaafar Mohammed, as "an advisor to Qassem Soleimani," the commander of the Qods Force, which is the external operations wing of the IRGC. U.S. military and intelligence officials accuse Soleimani of overseeing the deaths of numerous American soldiers and other personnel in Iraq. In June, Muhandis was pictured with Iraqi Prime Minister Haidar al Abadi and then photographed with

---

[4] Derek Harvey and Michael Pregent, "Who's to blame for Iraq crisis," CNN.com, June 12, 2014. (http://www.cnn.com/2014/06/12/opinion/pregent-harvey-northern-iraq-collapse/)

[5] Human Rights Watch, "After Liberation Came Destruction: Iraqi Militia and the Aftermath of Amerli," March 18, 2015. (Available at: https://www.hrw.org/news/2015/03/18/iraq-militia-attacks-destroy-villages-displace-thousands)

[6] Thomas Joscelyn. "Islamic State brutally executes 4 men in response to slaying by 'Angel of Death'," *The Long War Journal*, August 31, 2015. (http://www.longwarjournal.org/archives/2015/08/islamic-state-brutally-executes-four-men-in-response-to-shiite-angel-of-death.php)

[7] Bill Roggio, "US sanctions Iraqi Hezbollah Brigades and Qods Force adviser." *The Long War Journal*, July 2, 2009. (http://www.longwarjournal.org/archives/2009/07/us_sanctions_iraqi_h.php)

Abadi and Iranian President Hassan Rouhani during a high-level meeting.[8] The photos demonstrate the high degree of coordination between Muhandis' Popular Mobilization Committee and its Iraqi and Iranian government backers.

Needless to say, the PMC and its allies in Iraq are not substitutes for the "Awakening" forces that were crucial in turning back the advances made by the Islamic State's predecessor, AQI/ISI. Instead of clearing and holding territory from the Sunni jihadists, offering stability and governance in their absence, these Shiite extremists are escalating the conflict. The result has been that too many Sunnis who might otherwise prove to be key partners against Baghdadi's enterprise have either brokered tactical alliances with the Islamic State, or have not received an appropriate amount of assistance to fight it.

The situation is similar across the Syrian side of the border. Iran has buttressed Assad's regime with IRGC commanders and Hezbollah fighters, who are not going to drive Sunni jihadists out of their current strongholds and then provide stable governance in the vacuum left behind. It was Assad, we should not forget, who originally turned the peaceful protests against his regime into a violent conflict that has now cost more than 200,000 lives. Assad's use of barrel bombs and chemical weapons against Sunni areas are not a path to peace. Instead, Assad's actions have only continued to radicalize the Sunnis who are needed as a long-term roadblock against the Islamic State, Al Nusrah Front, and other Sunni jihadists.

Many have noticed that the Assad regime does not often fight the Islamic State. It is wrong to say the two never clash, however, as they have throughout this year. But it is true that Assad's war is primarily focused against others, namely, the part of the insurgency led by al Qaeda and its allies. The Sunni jihadists in this camp are opposed to both Assad and the Islamic State, but that should not make them a partner in any American-led strategy.

Al Nusrah Front is a regional branch of al Qaeda's international organization.

Although Al Nusrah Front in Syria is often called an al Qaeda "affiliate," it is better described as a regional branch of al Qaeda's international organization. It is one of several branches, with the others being: Al Qaeda in the Arabian Peninsula (AQAP), Al Qaeda in the Islamic Maghreb (AQIM), Al Qaeda in the Indian Subcontinent (AQIS), and Shabaab (Somalia). In each case, al Qaeda's regional branch is headed by a jihadist who has sworn *bayat* (oath of allegiance) to Ayman al Zawahiri and has agreed to abide by the strategy and orders set by al Qaeda's general command. However, each regional branch is afforded a great degree of discretion when it comes to waging jihad on a day-to-day basis. That is, al Qaeda's chain-of-command is decentralized to a certain extent. This does not imply a lack of cohesion, however, as al Qaeda's regional branches still openly follow the orders sent from al Qaeda's top-tier leadership.

---

[8] See: Bill Roggio. "Iraqi Prime Minister photographed with SDGT Abu Mahdi al Muhandis," *The Long War Journal's Threat Matrix*, June 13, 2015. (http://www.longwarjournal.org/archives/2015/06/iraqi-prime-minister-photographed-with-sdgt-abu-mahdi-al-muhandis.php); Bill Roggio, "Iraq's PM introduces US-designated terrorist to Iran's President," *The Long War Journal's Threat Matrix*, June 18, 2015.
(http://www.longwarjournal.org/archives/2015/06/iraqs-pm-introduces-us-designated-terrorist-to-irans-president.php)

Abu Muhammad al Julani, Al Nusrah's leader, is a regional emir in al Qaeda's organization. Julani was originally a subordinate to Abu Bakr al Baghdadi, but he helped establish his own group, in part, by defying Baghdadi's attempts to keep Al Nusrah under his thumb. When Julani refused Baghdadi's April 2013 order to fold Al Nusrah under the Islamic State, Julani publicly reaffirmed his direct allegiance to Zawahiri. Julani does not hide the fact that he follows the "orders" and "directives" of Zawahiri to this day.[9] Al Qaeda bolstered Al Nusrah by sending a cadre of veterans to join its ranks.[10]

Al Qaeda is seeking to build an Islamic emirate (state) in Syria, but has a very different strategy for doing so.

It is commonly assumed that al Qaeda is only interested in striking the West, and does not seek to resurrect an Islamic caliphate, or build emirates. But this is false. Osama bin Laden's private discourse and public statements are littered with references to al Qaeda's desire to build Islamic emirates and, eventually, a caliphate. The same is true for Ayman al Zawahiri, bin Laden's successor. Al Qaeda has consistently supported the Taliban's "Islamic Emirate of Afghanistan," believing that it is poised for a comeback as Western forces draw down from the country. In Syria, and elsewhere, al Qaeda is pursuing a strategy that is focused on long-term nation building.

Gradual implementation of sharia. As we've consistently warned at *The Long War Journal*, al Qaeda knows that most Muslims do not favor its radical version of sharia law. So al Qaeda's leaders have taken steps to gradually implement sharia in the areas under its control. This is radically different from the Islamic State, which has fetishized *hudud* punishments, graphically displaying stonings, limb amputations, beheadings, and other grotesque executions (such as throwing "gay" men off of the top of tall buildings) in its propaganda. An al Qaeda veteran known as Abu Firas al Suri, who serves on Al Nusrah's shura council and was formerly its public spokesman, critiqued the Islamic State's approach in a recent interview. Al Suri accused the Islamic State and its supporters of confusing *hudud* punishments for the totality of sharia law, pointing out that there is more to the implementation of sharia than just lopping off a few limbs. Al Qaeda believes that *hudud* and other aspects of sharia should be fully implemented, but various factors necessitate a more gradual process for reorganizing society along these lines. Al Qaeda has concluded that fully implementing sharia before the population is ready risks alienating would-be supporters. Society needs to be re-educated as to the "correct" Islamic laws, al Qaeda believes. Al Nusrah and other like-minded jihadists have, therefore, established schools for spreading their ideology throughout Syria.

An "erupting jihadi center." Indeed, this remains one of al Qaeda's chief aims: to spread the

---

[9] Thomas Joscelyn, "Al Nusrah Front 'committed' to Ayman al Zawahiri's 'orders'," *The Long War Journal*, May 29, 2015. (http://www.longwarjournal.org/archives/2015/05/analysis-al-nusrah-front-committed-to-ayman-al-zawahiris-orders.php)
[10] Leaders such as Sanafi al Nasri, Abu Sulayman al Muhajir, Abu Hammam al Suri, Sami al Uraydi, Abu Ammar al Sham, Abu Firas al Suri, have dossiers that stretch back long before the creation of Al Nusrah. In addition, jihadists online have claimed that Ahmad Salama Mabruk has relocated to Syria and serves on Al Nusrah's shura council.

salafi-jihadist ideology that motivates its terrorism and violence. As the aforementioned Abu Firas al Suri explained in an Al Nusrah propaganda documentary released earlier this year ("The Heirs of Glory"), al Qaeda seeks to spark revolutions throughout the Muslim-majority world. For decades after the fall of the caliphate, the "concept of jihad in the Levant was absent from people's minds," Abu Firas said in the video. "Nobody even heard of the word *jihad*. In reality, the Levant is regarded [as] one of the most important centers in the Islamic world due to its close proximity to Palestine, to the Hijaz [Saudi Arabia] and being in the center of the Islamic world." Abu Firas then introduced viewers to the concept of an "erupting jihadi center," not just in the Levant, but elsewhere. And he drew on Marxist thinking to explain what he means.

"The existence of a continually erupting jihadi center in the Levant is critical so people continue to hear about jihad," Abu Firas said. "Even western theorists, such as Frenchman Regis Debray, author of 'Revolution in the Revolution,' confirm the necessity of a continually erupting center for revolutions." Debray's book dealt with guerrilla warfare, especially in Latin America, and the revolutionary approaches employed by leftwing radicals in the mid-20th century. Abu Firas was quick to say that "obviously" Debray "is not our role model or example, nor [Fidel] Castro, nor [Che] Guevara, but rather this is a fact." By this he meant that no leftwing Western intellectual or Marxist can serve as the jihadists' "role model." But his explanation of revolutionary theory is telling, as it is known from various sources that al Qaeda has studied Che Guevara, Mao and other political revolutionaries in order to better understand their successes and failures.

Embedded within the Syrian insurgency. Consistent with al Qaeda's revolutionary approach, Al Nusrah has embedded itself deeply within the anti-Assad insurgency, seeking to win popular support for its ideology by becoming indispensable to the fight against an unpopular regime. In insurgent terms, this might be called a "bottom-up" approach, which is designed to garner wider support from the Syrian population. This stands in stark contrast to the Islamic State's "top-down" authoritarianism, which demands that everyone, including other jihadists, submit to Baghdadi as the "Emir of the Faithful." Al Nusrah's strategy has borne fruit. When the U.S. moved to designate Al Nusrah as a terrorist organization, other non-jihadist rebel groups vehemently objected. Such was the popularity of Al Qaeda's effort at the time. Zawahiri himself made this point in a recently "leaked" letter (written in September 2013) rebuking the Islamic State's leadership. Indeed, Zawahiri had ordered Al Nusrah and other groups to keep their al Qaeda identity a secret at first – all the better to avoid Western scrutiny and increase the jihadists' connection to the people.

In addition to Al Nusrah, there are various other jihadist groups in Syria that maintain some degree of affiliation with al Qaeda, even if the exact nature of the relationship is not altogether clear to outside observers. For instance, Jund al Aqsa is almost certainly an al Qaeda front. Jaish al Muhajireen wal Ansar (JMWA, or "the Army of the Emigrants and Helpers"), which merged with Al Nusrah earlier this month, was linked to al Qaeda prior to being folded into Al Nusrah. The same is true for Ansar al Din, a coalition that until recently included JMWA. The Turkistan Islamic Party, Uzbek groups, Chechens belonging to an arm of the Islamic Caucasus Emirate, and others all have demonstrable ties to al Qaeda's international network. And then there is Ahrar al Sham, a powerful rebel organization that has had al Qaeda veterans in its most senior ranks. Al Qaeda's desire to hide its hand in these and other groups is entirely consistent with its approach to guerilla war fighting.

Also consistent with al Qaeda's revolutionary approach, Al Nusrah has entered into a series of coalitions with other insurgents fighting Assad. The most successful of these, of late, is the Jaysh al Fateh ("Army of Conquest") alliance, which is led by Al Nusrah and its close jihadist ally, Ahrar al Sham. In March, Jaysh al Fateh captured the city of Idlib, which was only the second provincial capital to fall since the beginning of the uprisings against Assad. Since then, Jaysh al Fateh has cleared Bashar al Assad's forces out of a large portion of the Idlib province. From this position, the jihadists threaten Assad in both central Syria and in the coastal Latakia province, an Assad family stronghold.

Seeds of an emirate. With the consolidation of its grip in the Idlib province, Jaysh al Fateh has laid the groundwork for a potential Islamic emirate. As a leaked audio speech of Julani shows, this is clearly Al Nusrah's long-term intent in Syria: to create an Islamic emirate under which sharia law is fully implemented. Al Nusrah's "The Heirs of Glory" also explicitly underscores the importance of Syria to the jihadists' caliphate-building project. Al Qaeda and its allies still face many obstacles on their path, and their success is far from guaranteed. But it says much about al Qaeda's long-term strategic planning that Jaysh al Fateh has almost certainly captured more territory from the Assad regime this year than the Islamic State has.

Mr. POE. Thank you, Mr. Joscelyn.

The Chair now recognizes Ambassador Benjamin.

STATEMENT OF THE HONORABLE DANIEL BENJAMIN, NORMAN E. MCCULLOCH JR. DIRECTOR, JOHN SLOAN DICKEY CENTER FOR INTERNATIONAL UNDERSTANDING, DARTMOUTH COLLEGE (FORMER COORDINATOR FOR COUNTERTERRORISM, U.S. DEPARTMENT OF STATE)

Ambassador BENJAMIN. Chairman Poe, members of the subcommittee—is that better? Begin again.

Chairman Poe, Ranking Member Keating, distinguished members of the subcommittee, thank you for the opportunity to appear today to discuss the important issue of counterterrorism in Syria.

Many have spoken of Syria as the problem from hell. Today with upwards of ¼ million dead, more than 4 million Syrians in exile, a crisis in Europe and in Syria's neighborhood, and almost 8 million internally displaced, one can only say that Syria has descended to a lower and darker circle of hell. And as many have mentioned, from an American perspective, the enduring safe haven that has been created in Syria and in Iraq is an outstanding problem for U.S. security.

This hearing, moreover, comes at a moment of dangerous flux with the deployment of substantial numbers of Russian forces to Syria, and that appears to be a game changer for Western strategy. I think it's unlikely now that there will be any chance of removing Bashar al-Assad's regime, or of the regime being pressured to come to the negotiating table on terms that it finds inhospitable.

And I believe that it's important to look at the regional context, as well. While a diplomatic solution will have to be found, and there is no military solution has been said over and over again, we face a potential another round of flux followed by equilibrium at a higher level of violence with Sunni powers in the region supporting their proxies to fight against Assad, now backed by the Russians. And that, in turn, could raise the stakes from a counterterrorism perspective, as well.

It is a moment for innovative diplomacy, and I would just say that I share the view that we need to show more flexibility on the issue of the fate of the Assad government. And while, ultimately, a leader has committed the atrocities on the scale that Bashar al-Assad has, cannot be allowed to stay in power, humanitarian and counterterrorism concerns demand that we be flexible about the modalities of that departure.

As others have noted, the key shortcoming in Syria and Iraq remains the absence of a capable ground force which is essential for achieving the kind of success against ISIL that we seek to achieve. Here there are two critical problems; what has been mentioned, the weak showing on Equip and Train needs no further discussion here. But, equally, I think it's important to understand again the regional context, which is that our Coalition partners are far from engaged in this struggle as seriously as we would like. While Western allies are showing growing commitment, and we should all welcome France's decision to launch air strikes against targets in Syria, the Saudis and the smaller Gulf States remain principally interested in the sectarian conflict and Exhibit A in that regard is the conflict of Yemen, where a humanitarian catastrophe is also unfolding. And Saudi Arabia's determination to extirpate the Houthis in Yemen is receiving far more attention and resources than the effort to roll back ISIL and Sunni extremism.

Our and our allies' agendas are at odds, and that is going to be a continuing problem in this extraordinarily difficult situation. But that said, I still think that the strategy we have, while hardly ideal is the best one available to us. For all its grotesque violence, ISIL has not yet manifested itself as a first tier terrorist threat to the United States. It has not yet shown significant interest in out-of-area attacks. I believe that will change the more we bomb them, but for the time being, I don't think they can be said to be an al-Qaeda-like threat. They have not devoted the effort to long distance covert operations the way al-Qaeda did.

Much has been made about the threat of foreign fighters. I would point out that there's only been one case so far of a foreign fighter coming back to his home country and carrying out an attack. That was in Brussels. We see an awful lot of radicalization young individuals who want to be part of the team, want to show that they are part of this historic movement, but this kind of violence which remains low-level, and I would say non-existential, certainly, is the new normal in jihadist terrorism. It's not something to sniff at, but it is certainly less threatening than the catastrophic attacks we feared after 9/11.

I agree with Mr. Joscelyn about the importance of the myth of the Caliphate and holding territory. That has galvanized lots of extremists, but I would suggest that we have a number of tools at our disposal. We are seeing an accelerating campaign of drone and other air strikes that are taking our senior officials of ISIL. And I believe that over time this will throw the group off balance and make it harder for them to achieve their military or their state-building objectives. And I think over time that will also make a ground campaign more attractive to some of our allies who we hope will get involved.

I remain strongly opposed to putting U.S. boots on the ground. This would be repetition of the surge, and would only address symptoms and not the causes. I have a lot more to say, but I look forward to your questions.

[The prepared statement of Ambassador Benjamin follows:]

The Hon. Daniel Benjamin
Director, The John Sloan Dickey Center for International Understanding
Testimony before the House Foreign Affairs Committee
Subcommittee on Terrorism, Non-Proliferation and Trade
U.S. Counterterrorism Efforts in Syria: A Winning Strategy?
September 29, 2015

Chairman Poe, Ranking Member Keating, Distinguished Members of the Subcommittee:

I want to thank you for the opportunity to appear before you today to discuss the important issue of counterterrorism strategy and Syria. Today, the phrase that comes to mind – and that has been used by many, many analysts – is that Syria now is "the problem from hell." Today, with upwards of a quarter of a million dead, more than four million Syrians now in exile – causing a crisis in Europe and for Syria's neighbors – and almost eight million internally displaced, and extremist groups such as ISIL and Jabhat al-Nusra deeply dug in, one can only say that Syria has descended to a lower and darker circle of hell.

From an American perspective, one of the most worrisome aspects of the situation in Syria is the persistence of the safe haven that has been created there and in Iraq for jihadist terrorists. This safe haven, together with the experience of irregular warfare that members of ISIL, al-Nusra and others are receiving, along with the continuing influx of aspiring foreign fighters, makes undoubtedly for a deeply worrisome spectacle.

This hearing, moreover, occurs at a moment of dangerous flux. The deployment of substantial numbers of Russian forces to Syria appears to be a game changer for Western strategy. We do not yet have a full understanding of Russian motives or goals, but it seems fair to say that the deployment has likely dashed any hopes that the Assad regime would finally be defeated or even pressured sufficiently so that it would come back to the negotiating table. Russian engagement in the fighting or simply enhanced Russian backing for the Assad government will likely mean more civilian casualties. Judging by press reports and Russian comments, the Putin government appears to want to deal ISIL a sharp blow – in part, it appears, because of the growing number of Chechen fighters in its ranks.

While there may be some reason for encouragement and perhaps cooperation with Russia in the fight against ISIL, it is important to reassert that no satisfactory military outcome appears to be in the making. Ultimately, a diplomatic solution will have to be found, and one that has the support of the regional Sunni powers. Otherwise, both the private donors and the national governments that have supported Sunni militias in Syria will respond to the strengthening of the Assad regime by pouring new resources into the fight. The conflict in Syria has repeatedly achieved equilibrium between rebels and government only to see one side or the other raise the stakes – a move inevitably matched by the other side. We cannot rule out that this will happen again if the Russian move is solely about strengthening Assad and weakening his enemies.

For these reasons, we need to engage the Russians constructively – no easy task given the tensions in the bilateral relationship due primarily to Russian aggression in Ukraine. We need to urge them to show restraint in their actions Syria and to harness their efforts to achieve a return to the negotiating table. It is truly a moment for innovative diplomacy, and in this regard, I share the view that we need to show more flexibility on the issue of the fate of the Assad government. While ultimately, a leader who has committed atrocities on the scale that Bashar al-Assad cannot be allowed to stay in power indefinitely, humanitarian and counterterrorism concerns demand that we be flexible about the modalities of his eventual departure.

To focus more specifically on counterterrorism issues, I believe efforts by the US-led coalition in Operation Inherent Resolve are achieving some progress toward degrading and defeating ISIL, but clearly not as much as hoped for. The key shortcoming is the absence of a capable ground force, which is essential for achieving the kind of success against ISIL necessary to reduce the long-term regional and terrorist threat.

Here there are two critical problems. First is the weak showing of the U.S. equip-and-train program that aims to put Syrian moderates in the field against ISIL. The shortcomings of this program have been laid out in great detail in the press and hardly need more elaboration here. Obviously, the cost-benefit ratio of the program to date is not encouraging to say the least. It may be that given the vetting standards we have set, reliable fighters are simply not available – that the polarization has gone too far, and that too many human rights abuses have been committed. Nonetheless, it would still be my recommendation that the Department of Defense push forward with the effort. We may yet learn that the problems lay elsewhere, and we could yet find ourselves in a position of wanting to have a US-trained force on the ground. In light of the way the Syrian civil war has unfolded, one would have to assume that the conflict could go on for quite a while. Against this backdrop, an investment in training still makes sense.

The second, and to my mind greater concern, is that our coalition partners are far from engaged as seriously as we would like. Our Western allies are showing growing commitment, and we should all welcome France's decision to launch air strikes against targets in Syria. Our regional allies however are mostly focused elsewhere. The Saudis and the smaller Gulf states remain principally interested in what we habitually call the sectarian conflict, even if one important dimension of it concerns rival states as much as contending religious sects. Exhibit A in this regard is the conflict in Yemen, where a humanitarian catastrophe is unfolding. Saudi Arabia's determination to extirpate the Houthis in Yemen is receiving far more attention and resources than the effort to roll back ISIL and Sunni extremism.

In short, our and our regional allies' agendas are at odds. They want to eliminate what they see – questionably in my view – as Iran's foothold on the Arabian Peninsula in Yemen. They also are still eager to see Assad driven from Damascus and that capital returned to the Sunni fold after many decades – and perhaps as a payback for the Shia ascendancy in Baghdad. The Gulf States believe ISIL can be dealt with afterward. We have prioritized the fight against ISIL, but, as the statistics on coalition airstrikes show clearly, the regional partners are making very limited contributions. The sole bright spot in this picture has been the positive showing of the Syrian Kurdish forces of the YPG. But that group's area of operations is limited, and impressive as it has been in action, it is not capable of taking on ISIL over a broad territory.

Overall, this state of play does not bode well for our near-term prospects. Yet despite all this bad news, I believe the Administration's strategy for Syria remains very nearly the best available in an extraordinarily difficult situation. Over the long term, the threat of terrorism against the United States and its allies will be reduced. I make this claim for the following reasons:

ISIL is an extraordinarily barbaric group. Yet for all its grotesque violence – the decapitations, immolations, sexual violence and the like – it has yet to manifest itself as a first tier terrorist threat to the United States. To the best of my knowledge, although ISIL has called upon followers to carry out acts of "individual jihad" much as the late AQAP operative Anwar al-Awlaki did, no terrorist conspiracy of note has yet been attempted in the United States with ISIL command and control. The same is true of Jabhat al-Nusra.

To date, ISIL has demonstrated little interest in out-of-area attacks. Law enforcement agencies around the world have uncovered little in the way of cell structures in their countries. Perhaps most important, the group's strategy thus far differs significantly from al Qaeda's: The focus is not on carrying out catastrophic attacks against the U.S. and other Western powers as a strategy for forcing us to withdraw from the broader Middle East. Rather, the group now is deeply invested in its agenda of sectarian warfare and the creation of its "caliphate". The origins of this strategy trace back to the group's first leader, Abu Musab al-Zarqawi, the approach has served it well thus far: ISIL's exercise in state-building has had a catalytic effect on the imaginations of a small segment of Muslim youth in a way that that bin Laden would have envied. The group will likely continue focusing on these efforts since they are providing the forces they badly need and have made ISIL the leading jihadist group in the world – the team that other jihadists want to be part of.

I want to emphasize that we should not expect ISIL to forswear attacks against Western targets forever, and already there appears to be increasing chatter about undertaking more attacks of this kind. This was to be expected once we commenced air strikes against the group. Still we should remember that ISIL does not have a track record of covert foreign operations or long-term efforts to acquire weapons of mass destruction, as al Qaeda did. Terrorist groups, like other organizations, have to choose carefully how they invest their time and resources. Thus far, the choice for ISIL has been warfare and terrorist attacks in Iraq and Syria. Developing more of an al Qaeda-like approach would be a serious and costly undertaking.

That kind of network approach is of course not the sum total of the threat. Much has been made of the danger posed by foreign fighters returning to their home countries – including the United States – to carry out attacks. Over the long-term, this is a real concern. To date, though – and the time period in question is not negligible – this threat has also not materialized. The shootings at the Brussels Jewish Museum by Mehdi Nemouche remain a singular case, though there is still much that has not been made public about the cell that was disrupted in the Belgian city of Verviers earlier this year. Although law enforcement authorities are aware of hundreds and perhaps thousands of returnees from Syria and Iraq, evidence of a major threat has yet to materialize. Indeed, there is reason to believe that, for now, the returnees from Syria and Iraq are mostly broken and exhausted and perhaps disillusioned. These are not the mujahedin who returned from Afghanistan, believing that they had defeated a superpower and were determined to do more.

There is, as we saw so tragically in the Charlie Hebdo incident and in others in Canada, Australia, Denmark and elsewhere, a considerable number of radicalized individuals who are eager to make their mark. Whether we look at the events of the last year, the perpetrators and their operations show clear similarities. These are essentially low-tech assaults and hostage-takings, carried out by local militants with little or no direct involvement from major jihadist organizations. There may be some hybridism – for lack of a better word – such as we saw in the Charlie Hebdo plot, with al Qaeda in the Arabian Peninsula providing target guidance in its online publication *Inspire*, and perhaps giving one of the Kouachi brothers some training and money years ago. But again, to underscore, these incidents have not involved spectacular suicide bombings or complex assaults on large targets like Heathrow Airport or Wall Street. They have all claimed comparatively low numbers of casualties. This kind of violence represents the new normal in jihadist terrorism, and while it is a serious security threat, it less threatening to our societies than the catastrophic attacks we feared after 9/11.

The typical terrorists in these cases have been extremists who want to be part of the action, but at home. The spike in the frequency of attacks has been driven in part by the excitement of radical Islamists in the wake of ISIL's successes in capturing and holding territory in Iraq and Syria and the group's effort to create an independent caliphate. After almost a decade and a half of setbacks to al Qaeda, ISIL's capture of Mosul and control of territory from outside Aleppo to Ramadi has provided extremists with a powerful sense that history is turning their way.

(It is worth noting that even before ISIL captured extremists' attention, the new trend in terrorism was becoming clear, though attacks were less frequent. Early cases included the 2009 Ft. Hood shooting by Maj. Nidal Hassan, which killed 13, the 2012 shootings of seven in Toulouse and Montauban in France by a radicalized petty criminal and the stabbing of British soldier Lee Rigby in 2013 by a group of extremists. The Tsarnaev brothers who carried out the attack on the Boston Marathon belong in this group as well, since they operated without sustained outside guidance and used the crudest bombs imaginable.)

The ability to capture and hold territory – which al Qaeda failed to do – has had a remarkable galvanizing impact. I share the view of many that our efforts to curtail this wave of radicalization would be greatly advanced by a major blow to ISIL. This would have a deflating effect and would create doubt for many who are in danger of being seduced by the apparent success of the group.

Unfortunately, in the near term, there is little likelihood of such a blow being struck – though the introduction of Russian forces adds a new and uncertain element. At the same time, we should not see this as a reason for despair or for discarding the current strategy. Although there is a debate over the quality of CENTCOM's assessment of the damage done by US and coalition forces to ISIL, the air strikes have undoubtedly checked the group's expansion and as they continue, they will destroy more ISIL assets, sap its strength and make a real breakout from the group's current boundaries difficult to achieve.   The reason this strategy should suffice for the foreseeable future is that the U.S. counterterrorism instruments that have been highly successful elsewhere are becoming more effective now in Syria and Iraq.

Specifically, in recent months, we have seen an accelerating campaign of drone and other airstrikes that are clearly based on communications and other intelligence and that have resulted in the deaths and wounding of a number of senior ISIL officials. Complementing these have been Special Forces operations that have led to the capture or death of high value targets and the acquisition of considerable amounts of materials with intelligence value. These operations demonstrate that the intelligence "base" necessary for an aggressive campaign – chiefly airborne – is being created.

Some would argue that given the numbers of ISIL managers and the sizable nature of its infrastructure, a counterterrorism approach like this will be insufficient to cause the necessary damage to ISIL. In response, I would argue that such a campaign would certainly not destroy ISIL, but it could cause senior leaders to spend most of their efforts on self-preservation, disrupt any terrorist planning that might be in the works and make it difficult or impossible to maintain high-quality military planning or achieve key "state-building" goals. This, in turn, makes an eventual ground campaign easier. I would add that I believe there is a good chance that one or more regional actors will eventually decide that ground operations against ISIL are necessary, even if they currently are focused on other issues. Degrading the group in the manner described above will certainly make such a campaign more palatable to regional militaries. A ground campaign will also become a more realistic possibility as the voices of discontent from within ISIL's ranks multiply, as we are beginning to see.

A few concluding points:

1) Putting a sizable American force on the ground for a ground campaign against ISIL would be a major error. U.S. forces would undoubtedly inflict real losses on the group, but as we saw with the 2007 Surge, this effort would be a case of addressing symptoms, not the underlying disease. Since we are unlikely to place troops on the ground for a period of many years, our ability to prevent the revival of ISIL would be poor. Given the regional context of sectarian tensions, that revival would be nearly inevitable. The job of maintaining stability in the region

and diminishing extremism must belong to the countries in the neighborhood. Moreover, a U.S. deployment that aims at destroying ISIL will still be seen by our Sunni allies as an effective defense of Assad. That can cause real and enduring damage to important relationships.

2) We should be open to the possibility of altering how we embed forces with units of regional militaries – especially the Iraqis. Former Under Secretary of Defense Michele Flournoy, among others, has advocated changes that would have U.S. forces in a more forward posture, able to direct strikes. While this is not a near-term likelihood in Syria, it may make sense in Iraq, and for the time being, our prospects for success against ISIL will remain greater in Iraq.

3) Turkey's role in Syria is critically important. The U.S. and its partners need to engage Ankara vigorously to ensure that it does not complicate the current many-sided conflict into anti-Kurd campaign. Ankara has already seriously undermined years of positive work to diminish Turkish-Kurdish tensions internally and internationally. Its current orientation – and especially its hostility to the YPG – could have a powerful negative effect on US interests. Turkey, like our Gulf partners, needs to be steered into a more effective fight against jihadi extremists.

4) Finally, it is essential that the U.S. do more to alleviate the current refugee crisis in Syria's neighborhood and in Europe. Both by devoting more financial resources and by accepting larger numbers, the U.S. can show real leadership and increase the pressure on other nations to do their part. The refugee situation now poses a growing threat to European institutions and unity. If it worsens considerably, our national security interests – in Syria, Iraq, Central and Eastern Europe and elsewhere will be critically affected.

In Syria today, there is no shortage of reasons to be dispirited. But I am persuaded that what we require above all is strategic patience and perseverance. We learned all too painfully in Iraq the costs of haste. I strongly believe that we have the time and tools to reduce the danger of terrorist attack, and that we will benefit from a strategy that is careful, deliberate and cognizant of all the technologies and political trends that will help us.

I thank you for your time.

Mr. POE. I thank the gentleman. I recognize myself for 5 minutes for questions.

Is it in our national security interest that ISIS be defeated? General?

General KEANE. Yes, absolutely, in my judgment. I mean, we are talking about—it is a national security interest for us for stability and security in the Middle East. It is in our national security interest dealing with our allies, obviously, who are being impacted by ISIS. And I also believe that ISIS left unattended will eventually become more of a direct threat to the American people at large, and I think the evidence is already there in terms of the fertility for something like to take place. Certainly, there is the intent.

Mr. POE. Ambassador Benjamin, did I hear you correct when— did you say that Assad, he's going to stay in Syria? At some—he'll be the leader, the President, whatever of a portion of Syria, or not?

Ambassador BENJAMIN. Mr. Poe, first let me just say, I fully agree that over the long term we want ISIL to be defeated, but I think that the key here is strategic patience, and that we should do it in a way that comports with our long-term interests, and doesn't result in another mistaken deployment.

As for Assad——

Mr. POE. Strategic patience, does that mean that we'd let ISIS get a pass for a few years, and——

Ambassador BENJAMIN. No, I think it means that we continue striking them and we've now carried out roughly 6,000 air strikes.

Mr. POE. Are you saying those air strikes have been successful in stopping ISIS?

Ambassador BENJAMIN. I think that they have done a good job at containing ISIS. And I think that containment, unfortunately, is the solution of the moment.

Mr. POE. Do you agree with that, General Keane?

General KEANE. No. Absolutely, that's not true. What has happened, CENTCOM has chosen to use activity-based analysis to provide some impact of what ISIS is doing. Therefore, we receive information that says number of air attacks, number of vehicles destroyed, and we haven't been counting bodies since Vietnam, number of people killed. How we come to that conclusion is beyond me.

What we're not doing in terms of the analysis that you're not receiving, but it is inside the CENTCOM headquarters is a matrix-based analysis that looks at the enemy and says how effective is their command and control? What is their tactical and operational initiative? What is their territorial control? Has it gone up, gone down, where is it now? What is their capability to regenerate forces? What degree of resiliency that they have? All of those things I just mentioned, plus four or five others, are all to the plus, which tells you that the air campaign is not nearly as effective as it could be, and it certainly is not having any significant impact on those categories, which is the way we judge an enemy force.

Mr. POE. Ambassador Benjamin, without going into that issue more, I mean, I think the General is right, and you're wrong. This is not defeating ISIS. I would think they would applaud the same type of lack of strategy because they're expanding. But answer my question; is Assad here to stay in Syria, or a portion of Syria, now that the Russians are involved? Is that what you said? I'm just asking that question.

Ambassador BENJAMIN. What I said, sir, was that over the long term Assad needs to go. That, I believe, is consistent with our values and the revulsion of the international community, but that we should think hard about how we sequence that, and whether or not we agree to let him, for example, remain throughout his elected term in order to deal with the fact that the Russians are simply not going to leave ahead of time.

I also would point out, sir, that otherwise, we are right now in a conflict in which we're fighting both sides from a middle that doesn't exist.

Mr. POE. More than one side. Reclaiming my time.

Now that the Russians are involved, Putin, Napoleon of Siberia now moving into the area. You've got Russia, Assad, Iran now working together. How does that issue impact our strategy, lack of strategy, or a future strategy in defeating ISIS? General, you want to try that?

General KEANE. Certainly. Well, first of all, it is a reality, but we should not let Putin and his limited military capability that he's providing take us off what our strategy is, which is to defeat ISIS and put together an effective ground force in Syria to do that, and also do the same thing in Iraq, and provide the number of resources that we need to do that.

I would tell Mr. Putin that I'm going to fly my airplanes where I want, when I want, I'm going to do what I want with them, and you're not going to interfere with them period. I mean, the idea of deconflicting operations with Putin is ridiculous. There's no reason to do something like that. We have to stand up for what our goals are in that country, in Syria, and also in Iraq. Putin is playing a card here, and he's gotten away with it in 2013 on the chemical weapons, he got away with it in Crimea, and he got away with it in Ukraine. And given that encouragement that we've provided him, he's playing another one.

I do agree with this, Mr. Chairman, it does solidify what was happening to the Assad regime. They were losing Alawites, erosion of support not to the point where he was going to removed, but it was eroding, and the rebels were gaining on him, particularly in Idlib Province, and that was Jabhat al-Nusra. And he knew that, and that sanctuary that they have, that Alawite sanctuary was being threatened. The Iranians provided him the detailed information on that because their intelligence is better, and that's what this move is about, to solidify the Assad regime. And that will happen to a certain degree, but if we continue the momentum against the Assad regime and support that, and support issues against ISIS, I believe at some point we'll be able to work a deal to get Assad out of there.

Mr. POE. Thank you, General.

I yield to the ranking member, Mr. Keating from Massachusetts.

Mr. KEATING. Thank you, Mr. Chairman.

I want to touch on one issue, and maybe get back to some of the other issues we were discussing. I'll start with Ambassador Benjamin. What's the role of Turkey, Turkey as an effective partner? Within hours after the U.S. had an agreement with Turkish officials to use the air force bases to launch air strikes against ISIL, Turkey launched air strikes against PKK in northern Iraq, the Syrian Kurdish group. And the YPG has close ties to PKK, and is one of the most effective anti-ISIL forces in Syria. Plus, although they're improving, I think Turkey has also been one of the most— probably the most main transit site for a country where fighters are flowing into Syria now. What could we do to better work with Turkey? I think it's critical that they become an effective partner for us.

Ambassador BENJAMIN. Well, it's critical that they become an effective partner for us, but I would say the diplomacy with Turkey is an extraordinarily vexed problem, Mr. Keating. And Turkey has made clear that its number one priority is the removal of Assad. And complicating that is that President Erdogan has decided to essentially tack back against one of his greatest achievement, which was ameliorating tensions between Turks and Kurds in his own country by striking out against Kurds for political gain. And while we do benefit from being able to fly out of Incirlik now, we have an enormously challenging problem because the Turks are dead set against increased influence for the YPG, or any other Kurdish group outside of Turkey. So, the diplomacy there is extraordinarily difficult. And, again, the Turks are increasingly concerned about ISIL, but they are nowhere nearly as concerned about ISIL as they are about Assad, which has become an obsession. His removal has become an obsession for Mr. Erdogan.

Mr. KEATING. I couldn't agree—I was in Turkey just 4 months ago, and I agree with you that—in their hierarchy of their concerns, Assad is first, the Kurds second, and ISIL may be third maybe, so that creates a problem that I see. I don't know if any of the other witnesses want to see how we could better deal with Turkey, if that's possible at all.

Mr. JOSCELYN. I'll echo Mr. Benjamin's honorable remarks here about dealing with Turkey because I think diplomacy is very difficult to deal with them.

I'll say this, Turkey—in my opening remarks I highlighted Ahrar al-Sham as a group that's not our partner in Syria. They're a member of the Jaysh al-Fatah Coalition which is led by al-Nusra Front, which is al-Qaeda. Ahrar al-Sham fights hand and glove with al-Qaeda, al-Nusra Front throughout all of Syria. Ahrar al-Sham also happens to be Turkey's preferred proxy in the fight in Syria, and this is a group we profiled. I've probably written 100 articles on them about now in The Long War Journal, and there's no doubt about what Ahrar al-Sham is. This is a Sunni jihadist group that's aligned with al-Qaeda. It's being set up to be basically the long run Taliban in Syria. Basically, the al-Qaeda, at least pre-9/11, you think about having these local Syrian forces that could basically be a face for Sunni jihadism in Syria. That's Ahrar al-Sham is, and Turkey is the number one backer at this point of Ahrar al-Sham.

General KEANE. The only thing I would add is, listen, all the problems that Turkey has given us to be sure but, nonetheless, in mid-July they came to an agreement with the United States to establish, for want of another term, a free zone with us, and to enforce that free zone using air power. So, that is a beginning and a recognition that that will provide some relief in terms of sanctuary relief for people who need that measure of protection. And, of course, that serves their self-interest in terms of migration across their border with refugees, but it's also a way of protecting a ground force. And I think that's a positive thing, it's something we can work with.

Mr. KEATING. General, I appreciate your going forward with direct comments, but the difficulty I have trying to find out how to follow-through deals with the use of ground troops, as well. And you say that we have to have U.S. and our allies engaged in those ground troops to be successful. Two things; number one, how do we get our allies? The conversations I've had are not encouraging with our Western allies participating. Number two, let's assume we did, let's assume we were successful. What do you see for the time frame of those ground troops having to hold that territory?

General KEANE. The issue we have, and you mentioned in a discussion with the panel, is every one of our allies on the border there, their number one issue is Assad. And it's not that ISIS isn't important to them, but they want the focus to be the removal of that regime and what it's been largely doing to Sunnis, whose constituency is within their own countries. And that's why I thought the more aggressive strategy in dealing with Assad early on going back a few years, this is one of the lost opportunities we had to build a capable force that pretty much has gone by the wayside in a sense, because if you remember, a national security team from this administration offered that as an opportunity in the summer of 2012. We should never lose that focus, because I don't think they will participate as a ground force, an Arab Coalition ground force as long as that regime is there. But when you talk to them, once the removal of that regime, then they're willing to entertain the thought of taking some kind of ground action against ISIS, if it's still warranted at that time.

And I suspect, even though we should try some of these other options, and I think the administration is looking at some different options, I'm not certain those options are going to be successful.

Mr. KEATING. Thank you, Mr. Chairman.

Ambassador Benjamin was going to comment on this. I hope he has the opportunity to do that with other questions.

I yield back.

Mr. POE. The Chair recognizes the gentleman from Pennsylvania, Mr. Perry.

Mr. PERRY. Thanks, Mr. Chairman.

Mr. Joscelyn, what were the factors that led to the complete failure of the original batch of U.S.-trained Syrian fighters that crossed into the country from Syria in July, if you know, from your perspective?

Mr. JOSCELYN. What happened, and we were watching this, ironically enough, on social media. Al-Qaeda, al-Nusra Front has all sorts of social media accounts, and they basically were taunting us as this was ongoing releasing a statement saying that they had basically captured or killed a number of the Division 30 forces they're called as they crossed into Aleppo in northern Syria.

The problem here was that it wasn't thought based on press reporting that, in fact, al-Qaeda in Syria was going to interfere with an American-backed effort, which I think was shortsighted. I don't know who made that call, or who made that choice, but that's what it said in the press reporting. So, it wasn't ISIS that interfered with us, it was al-Nusra Front or al-Qaeda that did. And then quickly what they did was after basically intercepting these guys as they were sent into Syria, they then went and raided their head-quarters north of Aleppo, which we then—the U.S. then sent in air cover to try and kill them, and actually probably killed dozens of al-Qaeda fighters during the conflict. But the end result was that these 54 fighters that went into Syria were quickly disbanded.

Mr. PERRY. I mean, 54 is a pretty—what was the force opposed to them when they came in? Do you have any idea? I mean, 54, I'm just——

Mr. JOSCELYN. It's a drop in the bucket. I mean, the point is——

Mr. PERRY. You've got a platoon of fighters.

Mr. JOSCELYN. I mean, Nusra Front by comparison, and this wasn't even factored in the strategy, easily has thousands upon thousands of jihadists now if you just look at their operations on a day to day basis. And they're not even ISIS. And then you go deal with ISIS and all the other factors there.

Mr. PERRY. General Keane, in what ways do you believe the re-cent Iran nuclear deal with affect counterterrorism efforts in Syria? I know that's maybe a little bit of a stretch, but can you draw a thread for us and put some points on it that we can maybe see some milestones, if you can come up—if you can think of some?

General KEANE. Well, I think it's pretty self-evident. I mean, the progress that the Iranians have made in the last 35 years using proxy clients to sponsor terrorism for them, and also to execute military operations for them have led to significant influence and control in Lebanon, Syria, Yemen, and Iraq. And with close to $150 billion worth of funding that's going to be returned to their coffers, which is a significant percentage of their GDP, I think if we just estimate that likely 20–30 percent go to domestic needs to appease a population and keep them out of the streets, and most of it will go to their number one strategic objective, is not a nuclear weapon. Their number one strategic objective is to dominate and control the region, and that is where that money will go. And that will mean Hezbollah funding, it'll certainly means Quds Force funding, both of who are on the ground in Syria.

And I may say, making a significant contribution also on the ground in Syria but no longer there, but helped prop up the Assad regime before ISIS invaded Iraq was thousands of Iraqi Shia mili-tia that were all trained by the Iranians. So, that will be the main-stay of where most of the money will go. It will not just impact Syria, it'll impact other countries in the region. But, certainly, it will have impact on Syria.

Mr. PERRY. Keeping with that kind of a thought, the implications of Russian forces in Syria, and especially in light of the Assad re-gime's recent use of Russian warplanes to carry out air strikes. You kind of talked about this briefly before.

Do you believe the U.S. can still—do we have the resolve? What are the implications, what are the challenges to us instituting a no-fly zone should we chose to with the advent of Russian forces prop-er being in country?

General KEANE. Well, I think the free zone also would obviously be a no-fly zone. We would not tolerate the Assad regime bombing a free zone, so I think it's a—the no-fly zone has a little bit of a third rail to this administration, so I think a free zone is a better word. And, also, it's a place where refugees can go to seek sanctuary.

But look, what——

Mr. PERRY. Are we going to be mixing it up with Russian planes? Are American fighter pilots going to be mixing it up with——

General KEANE. I don't see any reason why the Russians would do something like that. They've got some intercept airplanes, they're called SU–24s. They've got some multi-roll fighters on the ground, and they've got some close air support airplanes. They have about a squadron of fighters, they've got about a squadron of Hinds and Hips, and they've got a half a dozen drones. That's a limited air capability. They've got some ground forces and some tanks, about a battalion size to sort of protect the airbase and the greater airbase—and a base they're forming north of that. That's not a power projective offensive ground force. You push it out so you don't have Jabhat al-Nusra lobbing mortars at their airbase and interfering with their operations.

It is a limited military capability designed to have significant political impact. And I believe it will have significant political impact. He knows what he's doing.

Mr. PERRY. Thank you, General. Thank you, Mr. Chairman.

Mr. POE. The Chair recognizes the gentleman from California.

Mr. SHERMAN. Thank you, Mr. Chairman.

At the beginning, I said that the Shiite Alliance was more dangerous, more evil, has killed more innocent Muslims, killed more Americans than ISIS has. What I should point out, what I failed to point out at the beginning of this, but ISIS is far more gruesome. Assad will give 1,000 people with barrel bombs and have the good taste to deny it. ISIS will behead a dozen people and put it up on YouTube.

There have been those who have blamed the United States for everything and said we've accomplished nothing. I would point out for the record that ISIS was on its way to take Baghdad, at least the Sunni neighborhoods in Baghdad, and it was American air power that stopped them. Speaking of Baghdad, this is an ally that may not be worthy of very much American support.

Ambassador, do you know how much money we spent propping up that regime this year? We've got thousands of troops there, we give them lots of free weapons. Any idea what the price is?

Ambassador BENJAMIN. I'm afraid I couldn't give——

Mr. SHERMAN. Okay. We'll try to find out for the record, but this is a regime that has oil revenues present and future that will not commit to repay us with future oil revenues. It's a regime that sends money to ISIS, it pays the civil servants in Mosul, which means they're giving money to people under ISIS control, it I believe gives Mosul free electricity for which ISIS can collect. But, most importantly, ISIS seized all those bank notes. The Iraqi regime will not recall them as many countries do and issue new currency. And, of course, the reason for that is that really makes it tough to be a corrupt politician because you have your store of money in the old bank notes.

We're losing the cyber war. The number one thing ISIS has is it does control territory, but the second thing is that our message in cyber space is terrible. One of the reasons for that is that we don't have anybody on our team who's paid to understand Islam. We think that if we can just prove that al-Baghdadi beheaded innocent girls, that that will undercut his support. It may increase his support. He may put that up on YouTube. What we fail to realize is if we can catch him eating a ham sandwich, that's what will undercut his support.

Ambassador, while you were in government, if you wanted to call a U.S. Government employee who's full-time job was to be a true expert in Sharia, in the Quran, in the Hadith, was there anybody who was a U.S. Government employee you could call on who had memorized the Quran, which is kind of a basic level of Islamic scholarship?

Ambassador BENJAMIN. Yes, sir, I'm sure there are many——

Mr. SHERMAN. Did you ever call on one? Can you name one, because I've been told again and again that the State Department refuses to hire anyone for their knowledge of Islam. Now, for all I know, our Ambassador to Paraguay is a devote Muslim, but he's focused on Paraguay. Who would you call? What office?

Ambassador BENJAMIN. So, if I wanted an intelligence briefing, I'd call the intelligence——

Mr. SHERMAN. Is there anybody in the Intelligence Service?

Ambassador BENJAMIN. There are many, many, many people.

Mr. SHERMAN. Who are true graduates of the top Islamic scholarship schools?

Ambassador BENJAMIN. No, but there are many other ways of acquiring that kind of knowledge.

Mr. SHERMAN. Well, there's many other ways—look, we hire thousands of lawyers at the State Department. We've got people on salary because they understand European diplomatic law of the 1800s. We don't have anybody who's memorized the Quran.

Ambassador BENJAMIN. That's just not true, sir.

Mr. SHERMAN. That's not true? Well, I've—can you name anybody who has?

Ambassador BENJAMIN. I'm sure that that's the standard.

Mr. SHERMAN. Okay. How about the standard of being able to apply both Sunni and Shiite Hadith to the behavior of individual actors?

Ambassador BENJAMIN. We have many people who can——

Mr. SHERMAN. We have many people, but you can't name one.

Ambassador BENJAMIN. I'm not——

Mr. SHERMAN. In other testimony from the State Department, they've said they refuse to hire anybody to do that. But when you say intel, that means they're not involved in public diplomacy.

Ambassador BENJAMIN. We also have people in the intelligence part of——

Mr. SHERMAN. Okay. So, you're saying the intel community advises our public diplomacy and our cyber communications efforts?

Ambassador BENJAMIN. Absolutely.

Mr. SHERMAN. That's an interesting role for intel to be doing on a day to day basis. I have yet to find a single communication from the State Department showing the hypocrisy and the failure to follow Islamic law of our enemies in the Middle East, nor can you name a single person that has this. But you're sure they're there.

Ambassador BENJAMIN. But I can show you 100 different pieces put out by the Center for Counterterrorism Strategic Communications that have done exactly that.

Mr. SHERMAN. Yes, and none of them by somebody who could— who would be mid-level at any of the top Islamic schools in the world. Yes, they've listened to the great course's summary of the Islamic religion.

Ambassador BENJAMIN. That's an absolutely unacceptable slur on some truly remarkable scholars——

Mr. SHERMAN. I asked you what post in the State Department is hired for their knowledge?

Ambassador BENJAMIN. I&R.

Mr. SHERMAN. IR?

Ambassador BENJAMIN. I&R, Intelligence and Research.

Mr. SHERMAN. Intelligence and——

Ambassador BENJAMIN. Also, NEA has expert——

Mr. SHERMAN. Okay. I've called over there many times and they've told me nobody, and you're telling me there's somebody, but you can't name them. And you know that they're only going to hire people with fancy degrees from Princeton, not scholarship from the major Islamic universities. But maybe there's some other reason why our cyber efforts are so pitifully poor when it comes to confronting ISIS.

Ambassador BENJAMIN. A major reason why our cyber efforts are inadequate, sir, is that Congress has never funded them at an adequate level.

Mr. SHERMAN. We funded them far more than ISIS is funded, and it's not like they've accomplished 10 percent of what they should have. It's not like you come to us with a success story and say we can do 10 more. We have the largest public diplomacy effort in the world, and the greatest failure in the world. And we are losing to people who behead children. We should be able to do a better job.

Ambassador BENJAMIN. Well, so this is a much longer conversation, sir, but the fact is that they have right now a story that is very attractive to disaffected Muslims in many countries around the world, and we don't. And that's a real problem. What would you propose that that message be? Come to the United States where you can't get a visa? What exactly should the message be to people who find that to be a really attractive possibility——

Mr. SHERMAN. Well, first and foremost would be a review of Islamic scriptures to demonstrate how what ISIS is doing is violative of them.

Ambassador BENJAMIN. Sir, the government——

Mr. SHERMAN. Giving visa to the——

Ambassador BENJAMIN [continuing]. Has done this over and over again and found out that when the U.S. tells Muslims what is Islamic and what is not, we fail.

Mr. SHERMAN. We don't have to do the telling. We can be beseeching those who can issue the fatwas, but we don't have the background.

Ambassador BENJAMIN. Do that, too.

Mr. POE. The gentleman's time has expired.

The Chair recognizes the other gentleman from California, Mr. Rohrabacher.

Mr. ROHRABACHER. Thank you. With all due respect to my colleague from California, who we agree with most of the time, I would have to say that certainly the cooperation between our intelligence services and public diplomacy are not only strong, but expected to be strong. That's part of their job, and I know they work with various people. I spent 7 years in the Reagan White House, and I don't think that they're any different now than they were then. There was a wide range of cooperation there with the intelligence community. So, whether or not they come up with the right policies or decisions, is something else again.

Anyway, I could go into great detail for you, but I was a speech writer for President Reagan, and I can tell you that there was a great deal of resources available on how people think in that part of the world, and what will appeal to them, et cetera, at least during the Reagan administration. I don't know, maybe they don't do that any more.

Mr. SHERMAN. If the gentleman will yield.

Mr. ROHRABACHER. Sure.

Mr. SHERMAN. I've called over there seeking information from people who would qualify as Islamic scholars and they've said, ''We don't hire any of those.''

Mr. ROHRABACHER. Maybe that's what they tell a Congressman, you know. Maybe they've got their——

Mr. SHERMAN. Well, they're really doing a bad job, or they're lying to Congress, and I'll leave it to our witness to tell us which it is.

I yield back.

Mr. ROHRABACHER. Okay. Well, thank you very much.

I'm concerned about a couple of things. One of the things I'm most concerned about is that we end up using our own money, and our own tax dollars that have been used in the name of fighting this horrible threat of radical Islamic terrorism. Of course, we have a President, I might add, who I don't seem to remember having been able to usher those words, or utter those words, radical Islamic terrorist, but I'm afraid that the money that we've been spending, that much of it has gone and ended up in the hands of the people who are radical Islamic terrorists.

This Third Force that the administration insisted that we support in Syria rather than going with Assad, which is what the Russians were proposing, I understand that that Third Force now is proven that it's actually now working with ISIL, and that some of their commanders who have been on the payroll up until 2013 are now engaged in activity with these terrorists. Is that correct? General, do you know, do you guys know anything about that?

General KEANE. I have no knowledge of that.

Mr. ROHRABACHER. Well, the Third Force just—yes, sir, go ahead.

Mr. JOSCELYN. The most recent reports are actually that some-
one in the New Syrian Force, a commander who may or may not
have been vetted to be trained, it's not clear to me based on what
CENTCOM is saying. CENTCOM's storyline over the last week has
evolved, but that a commander from this force may or may not
have defected to al-Nusra Front, which is al-Qaeda in Syria.

Mr. ROHRABACHER. Right.

Mr. JOSCELYN. Certainly, whether or not he was vetted or not to
provide—be directly involved in the program, he certainly provided,
according to CENTCOM, equipment and ammunition to al-Nusra
Front, which is al-Qaeda, which is U.S.-supplied equipment and
supplies directly to al-Qaeda.

Mr. ROHRABACHER. Right. Well, so there's ample evidence that
this has been going on. Maybe we haven't proven the case yet, but
I will just say that it—I think the idea that we should just create
a Third Force on our own and go out there and support it with people that we don't know, basically, because we're creating a new
force, I think has been a catastrophe for the stability of the Middle
East.

And let me ask about that. Again, why is it that you have
Assad—I mean, during World War II, we sided with Hitler as I
might say Putin acknowledged the other day at a speech. He said,
"Hey, you worked with us to defeat Hitler. We walked away from
being the Soviet Union, and yet you still won't work with us even
in the Middle East against these radicals." Why is that Assad being
a bad guy, but knowing that he doesn't intend to kill Americans,
why aren't we helping, going along with the idea of going over
there and helping the bad guy who wants to kill people who want
to murder Americans? That makes all the sense in the world to me.
Maybe we should have worked with Putin and it would have been
better off. If you want to refute that, go right ahead.

Ambassador BENJAMIN. Mr. Rohrabacher, I would make a few ar-
guments. First, we faced an existential struggle in World War II
that I think made collaborating with Stalin's Russia, an entirely
different proposition from collaborating with a mass killer like
Hafez al-Assad. I don't think that our vital interests are in any
way engaged in the region in the way that we experienced——

Mr. ROHRABACHER. You're saying Assad is worse than Stalin.

Ambassador BENJAMIN. World War II. No, I'm not saying—I'm
saying it's a different situation and, therefore, we should employ
different standards. But I think the other thing that's been lost
sight of here is that were we to side with Assad, or were we to put
a ground force into Syria to combat ISIL, we would quickly find
ourselves without an awful lot of our allies in the Sunni Arab
world, allies who we have long and historic relationships with, and
who we have many differences with right now, but who we still do
not want to fully alienate. And I would count among them Saudi
Arabia, the UAE, Bahrain, Qatar, and Kuwait.

Mr. ROHRABACHER. Sure, so all of these countries like the Saudis
who actually paid for the pilots to fly planes into our buildings on
9/11, we're worried about what the Saudis have to tell us. And I
will tell you one thing. At least you know these ISIL people are
right up front that they want to murder us. We put up with Paki-
stan, we put up with Saudi Arabia, and I think we are providing

or giving ourselves some sort of delusion about what the real world is all about. And I don't know what we've done to punish Saudis about what they did to help on 9/11, but radical Islam is our enemy, and the Saudis have financed it, and some of the very same people you're talking about have been financing ISIL. Have they not? Some of the same governments you just mentioned have financed ISIL. Isn't that correct?

Ambassador BENJAMIN. No, I don't believe there's any evidence that any of those governments have financed ISIL. I think that there have been cases in which some of them have financed other groups that we would consider too extremist for our support——

Mr. ROHRABACHER. Who then became ISIL.

Ambassador BENJAMIN. What?

Mr. ROHRABACHER. Who then became ISIL. Anyway, it's a very complicated—this is a complicated world. It's not something that can be just done with slogans. I understand that, and we need all the guidance we can get, and all the information. The General and I had a good talk out in the ante room beforehand about his various ways of analyzing a situation, which I found to be very helpful, and thank you. I had to go into the backroom with—we had a meeting with the Japanese, a Japanese delegation I had to meet with. I will read your testimony and look at it. Thank you for your advice today. And thank you, Mr. Chairman.

Mr. POE. I thank the gentleman.

The Chair will recognize a member not of this committee, but certainly welcome to ask questions, Ms. Sheila Jackson Lee from Texas, for 5 minutes.

Ms. JACKSON LEE. Thank you, Mr. Chairman, very much, and to the ranking member. And let me thank you very much for convening a very important hearing. As a member of the Homeland Security Committee and Judiciary, and a former member of this committee, I've dealt with these issues quite frequently. So, I'm just going to raise questions based upon my following of this, and I raise these questions with Mr. Benjamin. And I know it's difficult to maybe give a precise answer, but let me try to probe that.

Let me just take something from speculation and news articles that the driving of the Syrian refugees, tragic. No one will forget the 3-year-old, the picture of that will remain stained in our hearts and our minds. Do you think there was a strategy to drive those refugees at the time that they were into Europe, which was not prepared even though the generosity of Germany was noted, to destabilize their resettlement program? I'm just going to start there, work my way back to Syria. Do you have any sense of how those refugees, the large numbers that they were, were coming into Europe at that time?

Ambassador BENJAMIN. No, I'm afraid I don't. I can't say exactly what the trigger was. There were a number of things that happened on the ground in Syria that I think convinced Syrians that the situation was only going to get more dire. I don't think that there was anything that was done intentionally to disrupt European affairs; although, I do think that some of the central and eastern European countries that were waystations for the refugees saw it in their interest to hustle them out of the country toward Austria and Germany as fast as they could.

Ms. JACKSON LEE. My concern, and I'll go now back to Syria. One, 2 years ago, many of us were supporting the Syrian American community, and still do in terms of if we were back one or 2 years ago about supporting that military that was the Syrian, I believe, military component that was against Assad, to provide them with the support systems that they needed. And, obviously, it didn't come full circle for that to occur. We now find ourselves with the vacant space or the vacuum in which ISIS/ISIL has been able to take up residence, take up violence, establish a Caliphate, and to destroy any source of life that we possibly could have.

Do you have a position on what I think the President has offered, is that Assad must go, but there is room for his leaving to be tempered, or to be, if you will, established through a process. Do you see any good intentions in Russia's effort to maintain that Assad must stay? And, of course, now not only is there a Caliphate, but Russia now has seemingly an open door in Syria. It certainly has assets that it wants to protect, resources it wants to protect. And how do you see that playing out? Is Russia going to be an effective partner? Is Russia's dominance of Syria going to be a detriment to trying to get it stabilized for the good people of Syria that I met when I was in Damascus and spent time there who want to come back and reclaim their country?

Ambassador BENJAMIN. Well, you've asked a number of very good questions, and some of them are hard to answer. I think the short story here is that we do not know the full scope of President Putin's designs in Syria. He has talked about putting together a coalition to fight ISIL. And I think that there are intense conversations going on as there were yesterday at the U.N. between the President and Putin on exactly this issue.

I think that it is important to underscore that Russia has long looked at Syria as one of its very small numbers of true, reliable allies. And that has been true for many decades at this point, so it's not entirely surprising that Russia decided to take this step to support this one very reliable ally.

And I think that the President or the administration, I should say, is making a number of noises suggesting that there may be more room for discussing the long game in terms of Assad, but I think it's quite clear that Russia is not going to throw him overboard any time soon. And we don't have a lot of leverage there to effect that. So, that is why I said in my statement earlier, that I think that, ultimately, because of the crimes he's committed, Assad will need to go. But I think that there's a lot more flexibility in thinking about how that might happen now in Washington and around the world.

Ms. JACKSON LEE. The General looks like he wants to answer.

General KEANE. May I respond to that?

Ms. JACKSON LEE. General.

General KEANE. That's a very interesting question.

Ms. JACKSON LEE. Thank you, Mr. Chairman.

General KEANE. First of all, the reason why the Russians came is because Assad for this last year has been losing territory, particularly northern territory, and particularly in Idlib Province, mainly due to Jabhat al-Nusra. And, also, he's begun to erode his political base in terms of the Alawites possibly thinking about

somebody else. So, a 60-year relationship with Russia, former Soviet Union, over 100,000 Russians before the civil war began actually lived in that belt, that Alawite belt; a base on the Mediterra-
nean, the only base that he has outside of Russia itself, he cannot
in his own self-interest lose the strategic interest he has in Syria.
It is his foothold in the Middle East, so here he comes, and he's
going to prop up this regime. That is the main reason he's there,
he's creating a bit of another narrative. It's about ISIS, it's about
propping up the regime.

And here's where I agree totally with President Obama in his
U.N. speech, because what that does then, what Putin is saying is
I am reinforcing the status quo inside Syria, and that means the
humanitarian catastrophe that we have been watching for 4 years
will continue because Putin is going to subsidize that regime and
make certain it doesn't fall. And, remember, Assad has been making war on his people for these 4 years. It's not just barrel bombing, it's systematic genocide, starvation in towns and neighborhoods, destroying every food factory that they can destroy, bread
factories, canned food factories, et cetera, 62 percent of all hospitals
he's destroyed because that's another way of killing people, if they
can't be treated, 70 percent of all ambulances, and now the use of
chlorine gas. It's a very methodical systematic way he's using to
kill his population.

This is what Putin is underwriting, and this is the status quo
that that President spoke about when he said, ''The carnage will
continue.'' That, I believe, will happen, sad as that is.

Ms. JACKSON LEE. Thank you both.

Mr. POE. The Chair thanks the witnesses and the gentlewoman;
the Chair thanks the members, as well.

At this point, this subcommittee hearing is adjourned.

[Whereupon, at 3:27 p.m., the subcommittee was adjourned.]

APPENDIX

Material Submitted for the Record

SUBCOMMITTEE HEARING NOTICE
COMMITTEE ON FOREIGN AFFAIRS
U.S. HOUSE OF REPRESENTATIVES
WASHINGTON, DC 20515-6128

Subcommittee on Terrorism, Nonproliferation, and Trade
Ted Poe (R-TX), Chairman

TO: MEMBERS OF THE COMMITTEE ON FOREIGN AFFAIRS

You are respectfully requested to attend an OPEN hearing of the Committee on Foreign Affairs, to be held by the Subcommittee on Terrorism, Nonproliferation, and Trade in Room 2172 of the Rayburn House Office Building (and available live on the Committee website at http://www.ForeignAffairs.house.gov):

DATE: Tuesday, September 29, 2015

TIME: 2:00 p.m.

SUBJECT: U.S. Counterterrorism Efforts in Syria: A Winning Strategy?

WITNESSES: General Jack Keane, USA, Retired
Chairman of the Board
Institute for the Study of War

Mr. Thomas Joscelyn
Senior Fellow
Foundation for Defense of Democracies

The Honorable Daniel Benjamin
Norman E. McCulloch Jr. Director
John Sloan Dickey Center for International Understanding
Dartmouth College
(Former Coordinator for Counterterrorism, U.S. Department of State)

By Direction of the Chairman

The Committee on Foreign Affairs seeks to make its facilities accessible to persons with disabilities. If you are in need of special accommodations, please call 202/225-5021 at least four business days in advance of the event, whenever practicable. Questions with regard to special accommodations in general (including availability of Committee materials in alternative formats and assistive listening devices) may be directed to the Committee.

COMMITTEE ON FOREIGN AFFAIRS

MINUTES OF SUBCOMMITTEE ON _____ *Terrorism Nonproliferation and Trade* _____ HEARING

Day___ *Tuesday* ___ Date___ *September 29, 2015* ___ Room _____ *2172* _____

Starting Time ___ *2:00 p.m.* ___ Ending Time ___ *3:27 p.m.* ___

Recesses _____ (___ to ___) (___ to ___) (___ to ___) (___ to ___) (___ to ___) (___ to ___)

Presiding Member(s)

Chairman Ted Poe

Check all of the following that apply:

Open Session ☑   Electronically Recorded (taped) ☑
Executive (closed) Session ☐   Stenographic Record ☑
Televised ☑

TITLE OF HEARING:

"U.S. Counterterrorism Efforts in Syria: A Winning Strategy?"

SUBCOMMITTEE MEMBERS PRESENT:

Reps. Poe, Wilson, Perry, Keating, Sherman, Higgins, Castro

NON-SUBCOMMITTEE MEMBERS PRESENT: *(Mark with an * if they are not members of full committee.)*

*Reps. Rohrabacher, Jackson-Lee**

HEARING WITNESSES: Same as meeting notice attached? Yes ☑ No ☐
(If "no", please list below and include title, agency, department, or organization.)

STATEMENTS FOR THE RECORD: *(List any statements submitted for the record.)*

TIME SCHEDULED TO RECONVENE _____
or
TIME ADJOURNED ___ *3:27 p.m.* ___

Subcommittee Staff Director

www.ingramcontent.com/pod-product-compliance
Lightning Source LLC
Chambersburg PA
CBHW081119280526
45787CB00007B/2897

*9 7 8 1 5 1 9 4 7 4 6 2 9 *